servicing small gasoline engines

servicing small gasoline engines

BOYD DAUGHERTY

Product Line Manager, Educational Products
American Machine & Foundry Company

HAYDEN BOOK COMPANY, INC.
Rochelle Park, New Jersey

7 8 9   PRINTING

74 75 76 77 78   YEAR

Preface

The primary objective of this book is to satisfactorily cover the field of small gasoline engine servicing as taught in technical and vocational schools. It should prove to be of value to the owners and operators of the millions of small engines now in use, and additionally should be a worthwhile reference for those employed as small engine servicemen.

Servicing Small Gasoline Engines opens with chapters describing the parts and operation of two- and four-cycle engines. Since more material is available on automotive carburetion and ignition, most books dealing with small gasoline engine operation treat these topics from the automotive standpoint. This shortcoming is reversed in this book, since carburetion and ignition are discussed exclusively for the small engine. Nothing is borrowed from the automotive world. Float, diaphragm, and suction type carburetors —their operating principles and service procedures—are covered in separate chapters.

Electricity fundamentals are presented to inform the reader on how ignition and electrical systems operate. Both removable magnetos with impulse coupling and those of the flywheel type are thoroughly discussed. Complete chapters describe the servicing of two- and four-cycle engines. Outboard motors are discussed with respect to their special problems that affect operation and servicing. A chapter on troubleshooting provides hints for quickly diagnosing common small engine problems.

The author is greatly indebted to the small engine manufacturers, as well as to those concerns producing carburetion and ignition equipment. Almost without exception written and pictorial materials were provided in abundance, with permission granted for use wherever pertinent.

BOYD DAUGHERTY

Springfield, Virginia

Contents

CHAPTER *1*

Engine Fundamentals

Each year millions of small gasoline engines are sold. Lawn mowers, garden tractors, chain saws, scooters, Go Karts, and electric lighting plants are all powered by small gasoline engines. Such equipment requires servicing and repair.

This book will give the technical background necessary to trouble-shoot and repair any small engine, acquainting the reader with the operating principles of large and small gasoline engines. This book is written for both the man who wishes to repair and service his own equipment and the man who wishes to operate either a part-time or full-time small-engine repair business.

The principles of gasoline engine operation are not difficult. Small gasoline engines are internal combustion engines. These devices convert the chemical energy of fuel to thermal energy, which is used to do work. In internal combustion engines, both processes essentially occur in the engine cylinder.

Basically, the small gasoline engine consists of a single cylinder in which the combustion of fuel occurs (see Fig. 1-1). The cylinder is closed at one end by a cylinder head, and open at the other. Within the cylinder are the combustion chamber and a piston. The piston is a small, close-fitted part which moves to and fro, or reciprocates, within the cylinder. In its motion, the piston travels from top center, a point near the cylinder head, to bottom center, a point near the open end of the cylinder. The movement of the piston from one end of the cylinder to the other is called a stroke.

The reciprocating motion of the piston is converted to rotary motion by a crankshaft. The crankshaft is the main rotating part of the engine, and an extension of the crankshaft generally performs the external work of the engine. At least two strokes of the piston are needed to produce one complete revolution of the crankshaft, one downstroke and one upstroke.

The crankshaft and the piston are connected by a connecting rod. The connecting rod is joined to the crankshaft at the crankpin and to the piston by a wrist pin.

The crankshaft and member parts are contained in a body called the crankcase. The cylinder and crankcase may be an integral unit or the cylinder may be attached to the crankcase.

In operation, a mixture of air and gasoline is admitted to the combustion chamber. When the piston reaches top center, the fuel-air mixture is ignited. An explosion results, driving the piston to bottom center and turning the crankshaft. The burned mixture is then discharged, a fresh fuel mixture is admitted, and the series begins again.

This series of operations is repeated over and over again in a fixed order, and at the end of each series, all parts of the engine resume their original positions. One complete series is called a cycle.

The small gasoline engine operates on either a four-stroke cycle or a two-stroke cycle. In four-cycle engines, the series of operations which produce power require four strokes of the piston, or two revolutions of the crankshaft. In two-cycle engines, the series of operations which produce power require only two strokes of the piston, or one revolution of the crankshaft.

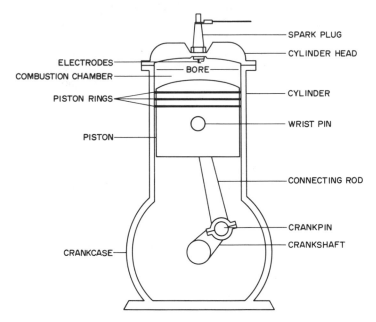

FIGURE 1-1. *The basic gasoline engine.*

Four-Cycle Operation

In four-cycle cylinders, valves admit the fuel-air mixture and discharge the exhaust gases from the combustion chamber. These valves are the intake valve, which admits the fuel-air mixture, and the exhaust valve, which discharges the waste products produced by combustion. The valves are kept closed by valve springs and are opened by cams geared to the crankshaft.

In four-cycle cylinders, the four strokes that complete the operating cycle are the intake stroke, the compression stroke, the power stroke, and the exhaust stroke (see Fig. 1-2). For every four strokes, there are two revolutions of the crankshaft, or a two-to-one operating relationship of piston to crankshaft.

In the intake stroke, Fig. 1-2(A), the intake valve opens, and the piston, which is at top center, begins to move down in the cylinder. As the piston moves downward, a partial vacuum is created within the combustion

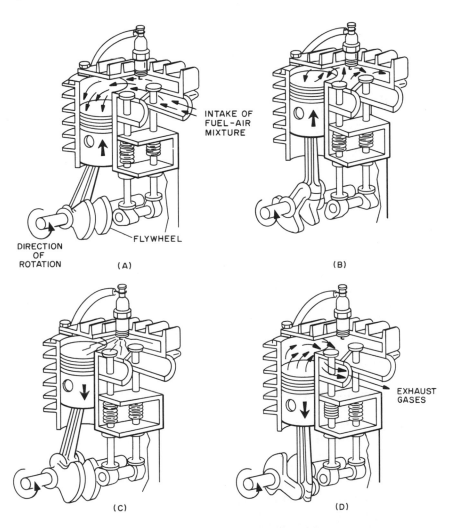

FIGURE 1-2. *The four-stroke cycle: (A) intake stroke, (B) compression stroke, (C) power stroke and (D) exhaust stroke. (Courtesy of Briggs & Stratton Corp.)*

chamber and a fuel-air mixture is drawn into the chamber. When the piston reaches bottom center, the intake valve closes.

In the compression stroke, Fig. 1-2(B), the intake and exhaust valves remain closed, and the piston moves upward, compressing the fuel-air mixture between the cylinder head and the piston top. As the piston reaches top center, the fuel-air mixture is ignited by causing a spark to jump the electrodes of a spark plug which extends into the combustion chamber.

In the power stroke, Fig. 1-2(C), the intake and exhaust valves are still closed, and the expansion of the burning gases drives the piston to bottom center. Near the end of the power stroke, the exhaust valve opens.

In the exhaust stroke, Fig. 1-2(D), the piston moves upward from bottom center, sweeping the burned gases out through the exhaust valve. As the piston reaches top center, the exhaust valve closes and the intake valve opens to admit a new charge of fuel and air. The cycle then repeats itself.

Of the four strokes, the only one to produce power is the power stroke. A heavy flywheel attached to the crankshaft provides the power needed to turn the shaft during the other three strokes. The flywheel stores the energy provided by the power stroke and releases it during the exhaust, intake, and compression strokes.

Two-Cycle Operation

In two-cycle cylinders, the piston takes on some of the valve function (see Fig. 1-3). In these engines, ports are used as valves. There are three ports: an intake port; a transfer port; and an exhaust port. The intake port opens into the crankcase; the port opening is covered by a reed inlet valve, which is a small, metal leaf mounted in the crankcase. During operation, pressure changes within the crankcase force the valve to open to admit the fuel-air mixture and then to close. The transfer port, located within the cylinder, and the exhaust port, an outlet leading from the cylinder wall, are covered and uncovered by the movement of the piston and require no valves.

In two-cycle engines, two strokes complete the operating cycle. For every two strokes, there is one revolution of the crankshaft, or a one-to-one relationship of the piston to the crankshaft.

In the upstroke, Fig. 1-3(A), the piston is moving upward in the cylinder, compressing the fuel-air mixture previously admitted to the cylinder and creating a partial vacuum in the crankcase. This causes the reed valve to open and admit a fresh charge of fuel and air to the crankcase. As the piston reaches top center, Fig. 1-3(B), the compressed mixture is ignited and the expanding mixture drives the piston downward, Fig. 1-3(C), transmitting a power impulse to the crankshaft. At the same time, the downward movement of the piston compresses the fuel-air mixture that was drawn into the crankcase during the upstroke. The reed valve is tightly closed by the pressure in the crankcase. In its downward motion, the piston uncovers first the exhaust port and then the transfer port, Fig. 1-3(D). As the exhaust port opens, the burned gases are discharged and the pressure in the combustion chamber is released. By the time the piston has moved sufficiently to open the transfer port, the pressure in the crankcase is considerably greater than in the cylinder. As a result, part of the fuel-air mixture in the crankcase is now forced through the transfer port into the cylinder. The piston head is shaped to deflect the incoming mixture away from the exhaust port and up into the cylinder. Thus, the incoming mixture effectively displaces the exhaust mixture and very little of the new mixture escapes.

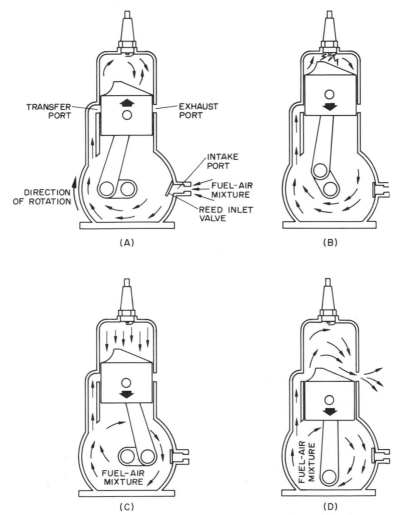

FIGURE 1-3. *The two-stroke cycle.*

Servicing Small Gasoline Engines

The momentum of the flywheel continues to rotate the crankshaft, driving the piston upward into the cylinder. The piston blocks the transfer port, then the exhaust port, and a new charge of fuel-air is trapped and compressed within the cylinder. At the same time, the upward movement of the piston creates a partial vacuum in the crankcase, opening the reed valve and admitting a new charge of fuel and air.

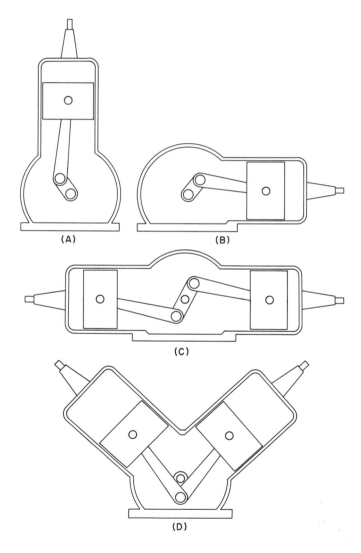

FIGURE 1-4. *Cylinder arrangements: (A) vertical, (B) horizontal, (C) horizontally opposed, and (D) V.*

Cylinder Arrangement

Engines are usually classified by their cylinder arrangement. In single-cylinder engines, the cylinder may be arranged vertically or horizontally, Fig. 1-4(A) and (B). In two-cylinder engines, the cylinders may be horizontally opposed, Fig. 1-4(C), or vertically arranged, one behind the other. In multicylinder engines, cylinders may be placed one behind the other in a row. Such a row is called a bank. Engines that have two banks of cylinders arranged as shown in Fig. 1-4(D) are called V engines.

Cooling Methods

The combustion that occurs inside the cylinder of the gasoline engine produces power and heat. The power produced is used to drive the vehicle; the heat produced serves no useful purpose, and if it is not effectively dissipated, the engine will overheat and damage the valves, pistons, and cylinders.

The two methods used to cool internal combustion engines are air cooling and liquid cooling. Most wood saws, lawn mowers, scooters, etc., are air cooled, while outboard motors are typically liquid cooled.

Air Cooling

In air-cooled engines, the heat produced by combustion is conducted through the cylinder and cylinder head to outside surfaces, which are in contact with the air. The amount of heat carried away can be increased by increasing the total surface area in contact with the air and by blowing cool air over the outer surfaces. Thus, in an air-cooled system, the outer surfaces of the cylinder and cylinder head are finned and the flywheel may be made to double as a blower. This is done by casting blades, or vanes, into the flywheel. In some systems, the vaned flywheel may be covered by a shroud (Fig. 1-5), which ducts the air from the flywheel to the cylinder and cylinder head. In some scooters, Go Karts, and motorcycles, no blower is used as sufficient air is blown over the cylinder during vehicle operation to provide adequate cooling.

Liquid Cooling

In the basic liquid-cooling system (Fig. 1-6), the cylinder is surrounded by a water jacket that contains water or another liquid coolant. As the engine operates, the water continuously circulates in the system, entering the water jacket near the bottom of the cylinder and absorbing heat from the cylinder as it circulates upward. The heated water then flows through an outlet to a radiator.

In the radiator, the water is circulated through numerous, slender, thin-walled metal tubes, whose sides are finned to provide a greater surface

FIGURE 1-5. *Air-cooled engine with shroud removed. (Courtesy of Briggs &* *Stratton Corp.)*

area. As the water passes through the tubes, the heat is conducted through the tube walls and absorbed by cool air blown between the tubes by a fan. The cooled water is then pumped back to the water jacket.

The amount of liquid flowing through the system is generally regulated by a thermostat, which automatically maintains the engine at the proper operating temperature.

On outboard motors, the liquid cooling system used requires no radiator. Water is drawn in through an inlet in the lower motor casing, passed up through an impeller pump, through the cylinder block and head, and then discharged. Here, too, a thermostat is generally used to maintain the proper operating temperature.

Lubrication

Proper lubrication is essential to engine performance and durability, for it reduces friction, and so, engine wear. In a properly lubricated engine, the mating surfaces of all moving parts are separated by a thin film of lubricating oil. If the flow of oil is stopped, rapid wear and early failure result.

Four-Cycle Engine Lubrication

In four-cycle engines, the lubricating oil is contained in the crankcase and distributed to points where lubrication is necessary by either the splash system or the pressure system.

A simple lubricating system widely used in small engines, the splash system utilizes a dipper, or slinger, attached to the bearing cap of the connecting rod. As the engine operates, the dipper splashes oil from the crankcase on the cylinder wall, the camshaft, the bearings, and other surfaces where lubrication is necessary.

As the amount of lubrication will vary with the oil level in the crankcase, some engines include a pump to draw oil from the bottom of the crankcase and discharge it into a shallow trough mounted beneath the

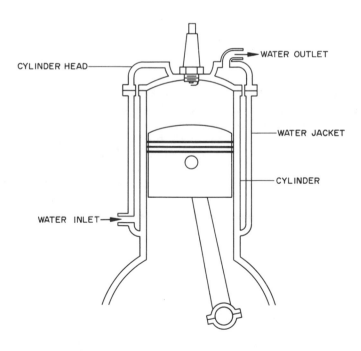

FIGURE 1-6. *Liquid-cooled cylinder.*

dipper. Thus, the dipper operates in oil maintained at a constant level.

In the pressure system of lubrication, oil is pumped from the crankcase to the main crankshaft bearings. It then flows under pressure from the main bearings through passages drilled in the crankshaft to the connecting rod bearings. Here, the oil is discharged through small openings aimed at the piston pins and cylinder walls. In such systems, oil is also supplied under pressure to the camshaft, timing gear, and other points requiring lubrication.

Oil Selection: Engine lubricating oils are specified by weight, which is an indication of the oil's relative thickness. Weights are specified by numbers assigned by the Society of Automotive Engineers (SAE); the lighter the weight, the lower the number, and also, the lower the temperature at which the given oil will flow.

The engine manufacturer recommends the oil weight to be used under various operating conditions. The recommendation is generally based on climatic conditions and the clearances of moving parts in the engine. Thus, 20-weight oil may be specified for a new engine in warm weather and 10-weight oil for the same engine in cold weather. After considerable wear, the same engine may require 30-weight oil in warm weather and 20-weight oil in cool weather. In any case, the manufacturer's recommendations should be followed.

The manufacturer's instructions also indicate how often the oil should be changed.

Two-Cycle Engine Lubrication

In two-cycle engines, lubricating oil is carried in the gasoline tank. Whenever fuel is added to the fuel tank, a small measured amount of oil is also added, so that the fuel-air mixture admitted to the crankcase also contains oil. In the crankcase, the oil condenses on the cylinder and bearing surfaces to form a thin lubricating film.

Oil selection: The manufacturer's instructions specify the type and amount of oil to be used. Most frequently, nondetergent, 30-weight oil is recommended. Some manufacturers recommend as little as one part oil to 100 parts fuel; others may specify as much as one part oil to 20 parts fuel.

CHAPTER *2*

Small Engine Parts

The basic unit of a small engine consists of the cylinder block and the crankcase. These may be cast in one piece or the cylinder block may be cast as a separate unit and bolted to the crankcase. Chiefly two metals are used to construct these units, cast iron and aluminum. Both metals wear well. The chief advantage of cast iron is its relative inexpensiveness; of aluminum, its considerably lighter weight. Of the two metals, aluminum is used more frequently.

Crankcase

The crankcase is the largest part of the engine. It maintains the alignment of the entire engine, and as practically all engine parts are connected to it. it must be a strong, rigid construction (see Fig. 2-1). Construction design varies considerably. In most four-cycle engines, the cylinder and crankcase are cast as a unit. The cylinder block and upper part of the crankcase are cast as one piece; the cylinder is closed at the top by a separately cast cylinder head and the crankcase by a crankcase base plate or oil pan. In other designs, the crankcase enclosure is completed by an end plate or by both an end plate and a base plate. In two-cycle engines, the cylinder block and crankcase are often cast as separate units, and the cylinder block is bolted to the crankcase. In these constructions, the cylinder and cylinder head are often cast as integral units, and the crankcase is cast as one piece with a removable end or base plate or as two, nearly identical sections. In the latter construction, the sections are assembled to form the complete crankcase. To prevent oil leaks, a gasket is sandwiched between the mating surfaces of the crankcase parts and between the crankcase and oil pan. The gasket consists of a sheet of fiber or cork.

Cylinder

The cylinder contains the combustion chamber, the piston, and usually the valve seats and valve ports. It is cast with either a water jacket or fins (see Fig. 2-1) so heat produced by the burning gases can be carried away rapidly. Aluminum cylinders either have chrome-plated inner walls to reduce friction and wear, or a steel or cast-iron liner, called a "sleeve," pressed into the cylinder bore.

The cylinder construction design is determined by the placement of the valves. The four typical designs are the T-head, the L-head, the I-head, and the F-head.

In the T-head design, the intake valve is on one side of the cylinder and the exhaust valve is on the opposite side. In the L-head design, the intake and exhaust valves are on the same side of the cylinder. In the I-head, also called valve-in-head or overhead valve, the intake and exhaust valves are located in the cylinder head over the piston. In the F-head, the intake valve is in the cylinder head and the exhaust valve is on the cylinder side. When the cylinder head is cast separately from the cylinder, a gasket is placed between the head and block to make a gas-tight, water-tight seal. The head gasket typically consists of an asbestos layer sandwiched between two layers of soft metal.

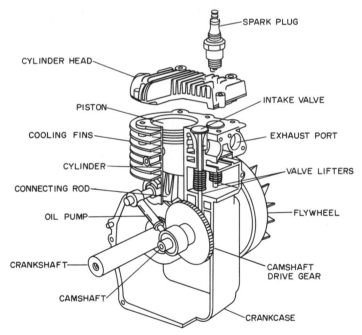

FIGURE 2-1. *Typical small-engine construction.*

Pistons

The piston has several functions in engine operation. It transmits the explosive force from the combustion chamber through the connecting rod to the crankshaft, guides the upper end of the connecting rod, carries the piston rings, and in two-cycle engines, also serves as a valve.

A piston operates under extremely severe conditions. It is subjected to the high temperatures of the combustion chamber and to considerable mechanical stress. It must be strong enough to withstand these conditions, yet light enough to avoid excessive inertia forces when its direction is reversed.

Pistons are generally made either of cast iron or aluminum. Today, practically all pistons are made of aluminum because its lighter weight results in less inertia in the reciprocating parts. This, in turn, results in better acceleration, safe operation at higher speeds, and a reduction in bearing loads and stresses on the crankshaft and connecting rod.

Piston sections include the head, or crown; the grooves, which carry the piston rings; "lands," which are between the grooves; and a base, or skirt, to which the connecting rod is coupled by a wrist pin.

Piston heads vary greatly in construction. The flat-head piston in Fig. 2-2(A) and the more complex piston head in Fig. 2-2(B) are used frequently in small four-cycle engines. The piston head in Fig. 2-2(C) generally is used in two-cycle engines. In this case, the extended central portion of the head serves to deflect the fuel-air mixture entering the combustion chamber so that it does not mix with the exhaust gases leaving the chamber.

During operation, heat causes the piston to expand. In aluminum alloy pistons, the piston skirt may be made with a split on one side, as shown in Fig. 2-3. The split permits expansion and contraction as the engine heats and cools, without danger of scoring the cylinder wall. Split-skirt

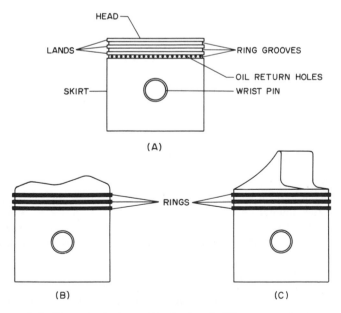

FIGURE 2-2. *Piston variations: (A) flat-head, (B) concave-convex, and (C) deflector-head.*

pistons are always installed in the cylinder with the split turned to the side of minor thrust. This is the side opposite the crank throw as the piston moves up on the compression stroke. Since the piston head runs much hotter than the skirt, the head requires more room for expansion. For this reason, some pistons are tapered so the head is slightly smaller than the skirt. Other pistons are not tapered, but the top lands are slightly smaller in diameter than the skirt.

FIGURE 2-3. *Piston with a split skirt.*

The piston must fit closely within the cylinder bore, but not too closely for it must be free to slide, and not too loosely for it will knock. The amount of clearance between the piston and cylinder depends on their design, the cooling system used, and the environmental conditions under which the engine operates. Generally, about 0.001 in. of clearance per inch of cylinder diameter is required, but in any case, the engine manufacturer's instructions should be followed whenever pistons are replaced.

Piston Rings

Generally, three or four piston rings are used: two compression rings and one or two oil rings. They are made of cast iron or steel and frequently are chrome-plated to reduce wear. Design varies, and construction may be in one or in several pieces. See Fig. 2-4 for a typical construction.

Piston rings are carried in the piston ring grooves; the piston lands between the grooves provide a smooth mating surface with the sides of the piston rings. The compression rings are installed in the upper grooves to prevent compression leakage; oil rings are installed in the lower grooves to control the amount of oil that passes up the cylinder wall into the combustion chamber. Generally, the piston grooves that carry the oil rings have holes, permitting the oil from behind the rings to escape back to the crankcase.

Piston rings must have sufficient tension to produce a leak-tight seal with the cylinder wall. Rings will leak when they are badly worn or when engine overheating has caused a loss of tension. In both cases, the rings must be replaced to restore normal compression and correct oil burning.

Ring gap clearance and the side clearance between the ring and the land are critical. Too great a clearance can cause a compression leak and oil burning. Too small a clearance can force the ring tightly against the cylinder as the engine heats, scoring the cylinder. Ring clearances may be checked with a feeler gauge (see page 99, Fig. 8-8).

Wrist Pins

The wrist pin connects the piston to the upper end of the connecting rod. Typically, the wrist pin is a hollow steel pin, case-hardened on the outside surface to reduce wear.

In some engines, the wrist pin is bolted or clamped to the connecting rod and moves freely in the piston openings. In others, the pin is bolted or pinned to the piston and moves freely to and fro in the upper end of the connecting rod. In still other engines, the pin moves freely in both connecting rod and piston. Here, to prevent endwise movement of the pin, lock rings are installed in the piston. In many engines, the wrist pin moves either in bronze bushings or in needle bearings installed in the piston or in the connecting rod or in both. In other engines where aluminum connecting rods and pistons are used, no bearing or bushing is used. Here, the aluminum surfaces serve as bearings. Wrist pins are not adjustable for wear, and when worn more than a slight amount, should be replaced.

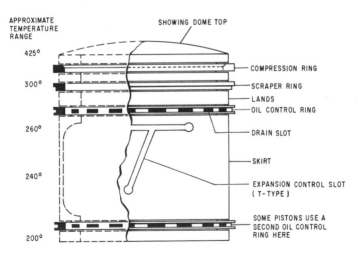

FIGURE 2-4. *Piston ring construction.*

Crankshafts

The engine crankshaft converts the reciprocating motion of the piston to rotary motion and also carries the entire power output. The basic crankshaft shown in Fig. 2-5(A) consists of the crankpin, the main bearing journals, and counterweights. The crankpin sits between the counterweights and is the part to which the connecting rod is joined. The main bearing journals are supported in the crankcase main bearings. The counterweights, or counterbalances, are located on the side opposite the connecting rod. They are either bolted to the crankshaft or cast integrally with it, and function to maintain the rotating balance of the crankshaft and to eliminate the vibration of the engine. The distance from the center of the main bearing journals to the center of the crankpin is called the throw.

Crankshafts are generally made of forged or cast steel. Most frequently, they are one-piece constructions, but occasionally two- or three-piece crankshafts are used. In all cases, the crankpin and main bearing journals are machined to an accurate diameter. In many cases, the bearing journals are then case-hardened to reduce wear.

The crankshaft usually has one throw for each cylinder. In a crankshaft for a two-cylinder, four-cycle engine, shown in Fig. 2-5(B), the crankshaft will have two throws, and the cylinders will fire alternately. In some engines, such as the eight-cylinder V-type automobile engine, opposing connecting rods are coupled to a common crankpin, and there are half as many throws as there are cylinders, or four throws to eight cylinders.

The number of cylinders in an engine also determines the number of main bearings. In small engines, there are usually two main bearings, a front main bearing and a rear main bearing. The rear main bearing is generally larger and heavier, as it also supports the flywheel.

In some engines, the flywheel and crankshaft are integral units; more frequently, the flywheel is keyed to the tapered end of the crankshaft and locked in place with a nut. Gears used to drive the camshaft may also be either machined as part of the crankshaft or keyed to the crankshaft and locked in place with a nut.

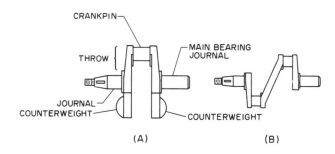

FIGURE 2-5. *Typical crankshafts: (A) single-throw, and (B) two-throw.*

Connecting Rods

The connecting rod transfers the explosive force from the piston to the crankshaft, which, in turn, converts the reciprocating motion of the piston to rotary motion. The two materials most frequently used for connecting rods are forged steel and aluminum.

The connecting rod is joined to the piston by the wrist pin. In some engines, it is clamped to the wrist pin by a single bolt, in which case the upper end of the rod is split. In other engines, the rod rocks back and forth on the wrist pin, and the rod is not split.

At the lower end, the connecting rod is joined to the crankpin by a separate, removable cap. In assembly, the rod and cap are joined around the crankpin and fastened by bolts or screws.

Bearings and Journals

A bearing is a support for a revolving shaft or axle. A journal is a rotating machine part (in engines, part of the crankshaft) supported in a bearing. The two parts must guide the rotation of the crankshaft in the engine, and certain requirements must be met in their design. Journals must be true cylinders, strong and carefully machined to resist deformation and to prevent excessive pressure in the bearings. Bearings must be rigid and self-aligning and designed both to take up most of the wear and to be replaceable. They should permit the crankshaft to turn with as little friction as possible. Bearing must also be finished slightly larger than the journals to provide a clearance between the two parts. This clearance must be adequate to allow for expansion as temperatures rise and to permit space for the lubricating oil.

In most two-cycle engines and in many heavy-duty four-cycle engines either ball or roller main bearings are used (Fig. 2-6). However, the simplest main bearing consists of an accurately reamed opening in the aluminum crankcase or end plate. The soft aluminum surface provides a low friction bearing surface for the crankshaft journal. In other engines, particularly those having cast-iron crankcases, the main bearings consist of bushings pressed into the crankcase openings. These bearings are made of

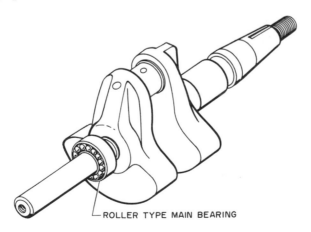

ROLLER TYPE MAIN BEARING

FIGURE 2-6. *Roller main bearing.*

FIGURE 2-7. *Bronze bushing main bearing.*

bronze, or occasionally, steel lined with babbit, a low friction alloy of tin and other soft metals (Fig. 2-7).

Two-piece babbit lined bearings are also used in some engines. The bearing is cast by pouring molten babbit into a two-piece bearing shell. Thin metal shims are sandwiched between the two bearing sections to obtain the proper clearance between the bearing and crankshaft journal. The upper half of the bearing is carried in the lower edge of the crankcase casting and the lower half is a removable cap.

To control endwise movement of the crankshaft, one of the main bearings usually has a cheek, or flange, which bears against a mating flange on the crankshaft. A slight clearance must be allowed for expansion. The clearance is adjusted by adding or removing washers placed on the crankshaft between the main bearing and the crankshaft flange.

An oil seal installed outside each end main bearing prevents the loss of lubricating oil. In two-cycle engines, the seals also make the crankcase airtight.

Connecting rod bearings also vary greatly. In some engines the connecting rod bearing is babbit. In small engines that have aluminum connecting rods, the relatively soft surface of the aluminum serves as a bearing; see Fig. 2-8(A). In both cases, two-piece bearings are used and shims are added or removed to adjust the clearance. In some engines, more frequently two-cycle engines, ball- and needle-type roller bearings are used (Fig. 2-9). In heavy-duty four-cycle engines precision insert bearings are used. This bearing consists of a two-piece liner coated with a low-friction alloy. By means of tabs, one semicircular piece is locked in the connecting rod while the other is locked in the rod cap. Insert bearings are not adjustable. However, they are very durable and can be easily replaced when worn by inserting new bearings; see Fig. 2-8(B).

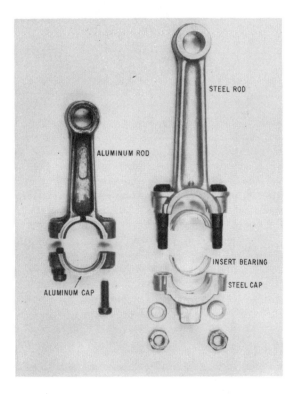

FIGURE 2-8. *Typical connecting rods: (A) aluminum, and (B) steel.*

The Valve System

Four-cycle engines require one intake and one exhaust valve for each cylinder. These valves play a considerable part in engine operation and function under severe conditions. During engine operation, they are exposed to temperatures of 1200°F or more; they must maintain a gas-tight seal in the cylinder under the explosive pressure of the combusted fuel-air

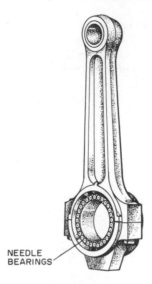

NEEDLE
BEARINGS

FIGURE 2-9. *Connecting rod with needle bearings.*

mixture, and they must open and close many times each second. If the valves do not open completely, and at the proper time, the engine will not develop its maximum power. If they do not seal completely when closed, there will be a loss in compression, and therefore in engine efficiency.

The most efficient valve available under such operating conditions is the poppet valve (Fig. 2-10). This valve has a mushroom-shaped head centered over a long stem, and opens and closes in a port in the cylinder head. The valves are made of special alloy steels, which can withstand the destructive action of high temperatures and the corrosive action of the cylinder gases. The exhaust valve is particularly critical. Unlike the cylinder and piston which are cooled by air or water, and unlike the intake valve which is cooled by the incoming fuel-air mixture, the exhaust valve is constantly exposed to high temperatures. The exhaust valve is therefore often constructed with a hollow center which is filled with metallic sodium. The sodium melts during operation, and as the valve moves back and forth, the heat from the valve head is carried through the sodium to the valve stem, dissipating the heat more rapidly.

The valves operate in ports or openings in the cylinder block. The stem extends through a supporting guide which is generally an accurately reamed opening in the block (Fig. 2-10). When the valve is closed, the face makes contact with the stationary seat producing a leakproof seal. A coil spring installed on the stem holds the valve closed. The spring is supported on the lower end by a retainer locked to the end of the valve stem. The lock, called a keeper, frequently consists of two C-shaped washers; these fit into a groove cut around the end of the valve stem (Fig. 2-11). A depression in the lower edge of the retainer fits over the keeper, holding the two sections in place. A second type of retainer, which is inserted

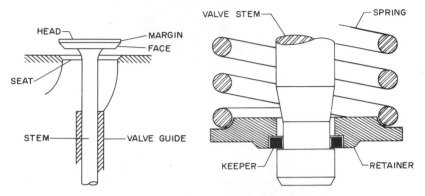

FIGURE 2-10. *Four-cycle engine valve.* (*Courtesy of Briggs & Stratton Corp.*)

FIGURE 2-11. *Valve spring, retainer, and keeper.*

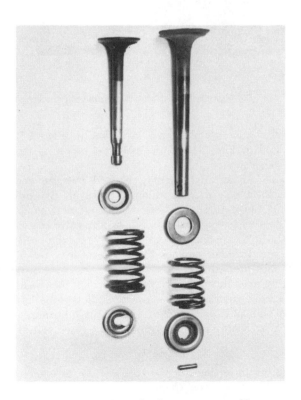

FIGURE 2-12. *Typical valve spring assemblies.*

CAMSHAFT GEAR

TIMING MARKS

CRANKSHAFT GEAR

FIGURE 2-13. *Valve timing marks.*

directly into the valve stem groove is shown in Fig. 2-12(A). In the arrangement used in Fig. 2-12(B), a pin-type keeper is inserted through a hole in the valve stem.

Worn valve guides are generally reamed oversize and valves with oversize stems installed. In some engines, however, the valve guides are replaceable; the old guides are pressed out and new guides pressed in.

In small engines having cast iron blocks, the valve seats are frequently ground directly in the cylinder block and are reconditioned by a special grinding machine. In other engines the old seats may be pried or broken out and new ones pressed in.

The engine manufacturer invariably specifies the clearance between the end of the valve stem and the valve lifter. If there is insufficient clearance, the valve will not close completely, resulting in a compression leak and a power loss. Even more important, the flaming gases will erode the valve face and seat.

If there is too great clearance, the valve will open late and close early, allowing too little time for the fuel mixture to enter or the exhaust gases to leave the combustion chamber.

The methods of valve adjustment will depend on the lifter used in the system. The first consists of a two-piece threaded lifter with a lock nut. The nut is loosened and the lifter is turned to increase or decrease the clearance. The second lifter is a simple one-piece lifter and adjustment is made by grinding the end of the valve stem until the specified clearance is obtained.

Valves must open and close at the proper time if the engine is to have optimum performance. As a rule the crankshaft and camshaft gears will have timing marks scribed at one point on their edges. To assure correct timing, the gears are meshed to the timing marks (Fig. 2-13).

CHAPTER 3

Carburetors

The function of a carburetor is to produce a mixture of fuel and air that will burn efficiently in the engine. The proportion of fuel and air required for proper engine operation will vary as the speed and operating temperature of the engine vary. The carburetor, therefore, must contain not only a system for metering fuel and air, but also devices which will vary the proportions of fuel to air as the engine operating conditions vary.

The main metering system of the carburetor includes a fuel system and an air system. A simple carburetor is shown in Fig. 3-1. The fuel system consists of a fuel chamber, a float, and a fuel jet, or nozzle, which is vented from the float chamber into the air system of the carburetor. The air system consists of an air tube with a venturi section. The venturi is a tube whose center is narrower than either of its ends. The venturi section in the air tube serves to increase the velocity of the air flowing into the system. As the velocity of air increases, its density and pressure decrease; the air pressure on the fuel surface in the fuel chamber is greater than the air pressure on the fuel surface of the fuel jet. The difference in pressure causes the fuel to flow from the fuel chamber into the fuel jet, where it is sprayed into the air tube.

The secondary metering devices of the carburetor include the fuel-needle valve, the choke, and the throttle. These three valves govern the richness and amount of fuel-air mixture reaching the engine.

The fuel-needle valve is an adjustable valve at the base of the fuel jet. It regulates the amount of fuel that flows from the fuel chamber into the fuel jet. Opening the valve will increase the quantity of fuel sprayed into the air tube from the fuel jet, providing a rich fuel-air mixture. Closing the valve will decrease the quantity of fuel, providing a lean fuel-air mixture.

The choke and throttle valves are thin discs mounted on shafts on either side of the fuel jet. The choke valve controls the amount of air passing through the carburetor. By turning the choke to its closed position, less air is admitted into the carburetor, which produces the richer fuel-air mixture required to start a cold engine.

The throttle valve, mounted at a point where the fuel and air have already combined, controls the amount of mixture that reaches the engine, and in turn, the engine speed and power output. Under idling or low-speed conditions, the throttle is almost closed; at maximum speeds, it is wide open.

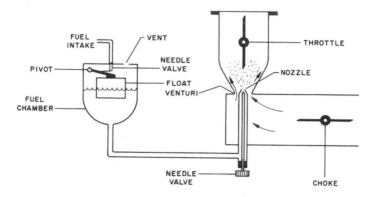

FIGURE 3-1. *A simple float carburetor.*

Fuel Level Control

The fuel level in the fuel chamber must remain fairly constant and slightly below the level of the fuel jet. If the fuel level is too high, fuel will flow constantly into the system; if it is too low, the air pressure must be further decreased in the air tube to draw a given amount of fuel. The fuel level is maintained at a constant level by a float-operated valve, called a float-needle valve. The valve is mounted on top of the float and positioned directly under the valve seat.

As the engine operates, fuel is drawn from the fuel chamber and through the fuel jet into the air tube, causing the fuel level in the chamber and the float to fall. As the float descends, the needle valve opens and fuel enters the chamber. The fuel level and the float now rise, and the needle valve is closed. Actually, the float operates automatically so that the inward flow of fuel to the carburetor is equal to the outward flow of fuel to the engine.

The fuel level in the fuel chamber must also be subject to the outside atmospheric pressure or a partial vacuum would be created in the chamber and the fuel would not flow through the fuel jet. Thus, a vent is placed in the top of the fuel chamber.

Fuel and Air Mixtures

The ratio of air to fuel produced in the carburetor will vary as operating conditions vary. When the engine is not operating, no air flows into the carburetor. The pressure in the air tube is therefore the same as the pressure in the fuel chamber, and no fuel will flow. When the engine is running, air is drawn into the engine and through the venturi, creating a pressure reduction in the air tube and causing the fuel to flow. As the flow of air through the carburetor increases, the flow of fuel will also increase. However, the proportions of air to fuel will change considerably, for as the velocity of air increases its density decreases, while the density of the fuel remains fairly constant. Therefore, during engine operation, the fuel-air mixture will progress from lean to rich as the speeds and power output increase.

The fuel-air proportions produced in the carburetor may not be the proper proportions for efficient engine operation. At idling or low speeds, a rich fuel-air mixture is required. However, at these speeds, when the throttle is nearly closed, so little air flows into the carburetor that little fuel will flow. Conversely, at medium operating speeds, the engine requires a leaner fuel-air mixture, while the carburetor is producing a richer mixture. Only at maximum speeds, when the throttle is wide open, are the proportions of fuel to air correct for the engine speed and output. A more sophisticated system is needed, therefore, to produce the correct fuel-air ratio for all throttle openings and engine speeds.

Idling Systems

The idling system is a low-speed, fuel-metering system which controls the flow of fuel until the throttle is opened wide enough to permit the main metering system to function.

In the basic idling system, a second fuel line, or idle jet, is vented from the fuel chamber to the air tube at a point near the throttle. Refer to Fig. 3-2. A high vacuum exists at this point when the throttle is in its near-closed idling position and forces the fuel to flow through the idle jet. As the throttle is opened, the vacuum at the idle jet decreases, while that on the fuel jet in the venturi increases. Thus, fuel will not flow through the idle jet, but will flow through the fuel jet.

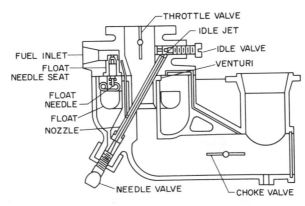

FIGURE 3-2. *Flo-Jet carburetor. (Courtesy of Briggs & Stratton Corp.)*

Although the basic idling system will supply fuel at idle and low speeds, it requires further refinement to meter the fuel and air in the proper proportions. Often, at idling speeds, when air flow is decreasing and fuel flow is increasing, the mixture may be too rich. Also, as the main system takes over from the idle system, there is an unequal increase in the delivery of air and fuel, and this inequality must be compensated for. Several variations of the basic idling system are shown in Fig. 3-3.

In the idling system of Fig. 3-3(A), there is also a second passage vented from the fuel chamber into the air system. The secondary, or idle, fuel passage opens into the idle jet. Here, however, the idle jet includes several openings into the air chamber. The first, called the primary idle orifice, opens at a point just *above* the throttle when the throttle is in its near-closed position. The second opening, called the secondary idle orifice, opens at a point just *below* the throttle when the throttle is in its closed position. The third opening, which sits below the secondary idle orifice, is also the seat for the idle adjusting valve. The idle adjust valve controls the amount of fuel passing the fuel passage into the idle jet.

When the throttle valve is in the idling position, the valve edge sits between the primary and secondary idle orifices. With the valve in this position, the air pressure at the primary idle orifice is lower than the air pressure in the fuel chamber. Fuel is forced from the fuel chamber into the idle fuel passage and through the metering orifice of the idle jet, where it is then combined with air entering through the idle valve seat. The mixing of air with the fuel helps atomize the fuel, and this process is repeated at the secondary idle orifice as the fuel travels through the idle jet. As this rich mixture of fuel and air emerges from the primary idle orifice, it is reduced to the correct proportions by the air which passes around the slightly opened throttle valve. The resulting mixture is correct for operating the engine at idling speed.

As the throttle is slowly opened, the pressure increases at the primary idle orifice and the fuel flow stops at this opening. At the same time, pressure decreases at the secondary idle orifice, which no longer bleeds air into the idle jet, but begins to feed fuel into the engine. This maintains the correct fuel-air ratio, since the throttle valve is now opened wider and will admit a greater amount of air to blend with this additional fuel. As the throttle opens still wider, the idle fuel system begins to fade out and the main metering system takes over.

In Fig. 3-3(B), an air bleed system is used to adjust the proportions of fuel and air to the varying engine speeds. This system includes a power jet; a power adjusting valve; a nozzle; nozzle air bleeds, or holes; a nozzle air vent, and an accelerating well. Fuel feeds from the fuel chamber through the opening between the power adjusting valve and the power adjusting valve seat, passes through the power jet, and enters the nozzle, where it is discharged in the air stream at the venturi. When the throttle is in idle or low-speed position, fuel rises through the nozzle and out the nozzle air bleeds to fill the accelerating well. As the engine speed increases, the air flow through the venturi gradually increases, reducing the pressure on the nozzle tip, and fuel flows into the air streams. At the same time, because the size of the power jet and the setting of the power adjusting valve limit the flow of fuel entering the nozzle, the fuel stored in the accelerating well will also be forced through the nozzle air bleeds and into the nozzle. As the accelerating well empties, air enters the nozzle through the air bleeds. The amount of air that can enter the nozzle is limited by the size of the nozzle air vent.

The air bleeds in the nozzle help atomize or break up the fuel into finer particles, regulate the quantity and rate of discharge of the fuel fed from the accelerating well during acceleration, and provide the correct mixture proportions for full-throttle operation.

In Fig. 3-3(C), the correct fuel-to-air ratio is metered to the engine at varying operating speeds by an economizer system. Here, the flow of fuel is controlled to provide the proper fuel-air ratio for the engine by regulating the air pressure in the fuel chamber. The system includes an air vent in the fuel chamber and a jet, called an economizer jet, which opens into the air tube at a point where the throttle opens when it is in the idling position. All the air that enters the fuel bowl chamber must first pass through the air vent. The size of air vent controls or limits the amount of air that can enter the fuel bowl chamber. The amount of air drawn from the fuel chamber is controlled by the size of the economizer jet, the economizer orifice, and the position of the throttle valve, as its position determines the suction at the economizer orifice. As the throttle valve is opened from the fast idle position, the economizer orifice is gradually exposed to suction, and air flows from the fuel chamber through the economizer jet and out the economizer orifice. This air must be replaced by air entering through the fuel chamber vent, but as the size of the vent restricts the amount of air that can enter, the resultant pressure in the fuel bowl chamber will be lowered, reducing the pressure differences between the fuel jet and the fuel bowl chamber. The flow of fuel, therefore, will be reduced so that the exact economy mixture ratio will be delivered to the engine at this throttle opening. Further opening the throttle exposes the entire economizer orifice to suction, and additional air is removed from the fuel bowl chamber, again leaning the mixture ratio to proper proportions for this new throttle opening. When the throttle is fully open, the suction on the economizer orifice stops, and little air is drawn from the fuel bowl chamber, while additional fuel flows to the engine, providing the extra rich mixture required at maximum speeds.

Figure 3-2 shows a fourth metering system. In this carburetor, the fuel jet extends upward and across the venturi and into the idle valve chamber. At the point where it passes through the venturi, the fuel jet has holes drilled into it. At speeds above idle, fuel is drawn through these holes. The extension of the fuel jet through the air stream acts as an air foil, creating a still lower pressure on the upper side of the fuel jet. This air-foil action aids the venturi in drawing fuel from the discharge holes. The fuel needle valve is used to adjust the mixture at operating speeds. At idling speeds, the fuel jet discharges from the jet tip into the idle valve seat which opens near the throttle. Here, when the throttle is in its near-closed position, the pres-

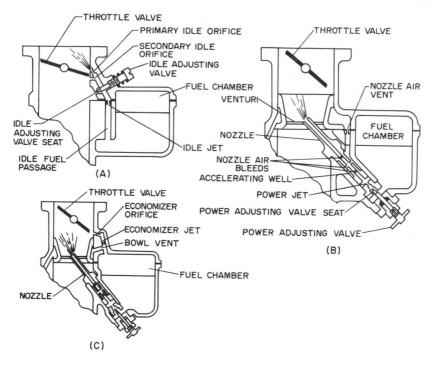

FIGURE 3-3. *Marvel-Schebler carburetor. (Courtesy of Marvel-Schebler Products Division, Borg-Warner Corp.)*

sure is low and fuel will flow from the jet tip. As the throttle is opened, the pressure decreases at the idle valve opening and fuel is discharged through the jet holes.

Fuel Tanks

In most small engines the fuel tank is mounted above the level of the inlet to the fuel chamber and fuel is fed into the fuel chamber by the force of gravity. Gravity-fed fuel systems usually include a fuel filter and a cutoff valve at the tank outlet. The filter restricts the flow of sediment from the tank to the carburetor. The valve cuts off the fuel flow to the fuel chamber, making it unnecessary to drain the fuel tank when removing the carburetor for servicing.

In some small engines, the most convenient location for the fuel tank is at the point below the inlet to the fuel chamber, and the fuel is pumped to the fuel chamber. Diaphragm fuel pumps are generally used. On four-cycle engines, the pump is driven by the engine camshaft; in two-cycle engines, the fuel-pump diaphragm is exposed on one side to the crankcase pressure pulsations, where the variations in crankcase pressure flex the pump diaphragm.

Floatless Carburetors

Float carburetors do not operate properly when tilted acutely from normal operating positions. For this reason, floatless carburetors were developed for equipment such as chain saws where the engine must operate throughout a wide range of positions. Floatless carburetors will operate continuously at acute angles and for short times while inverted. There are two forms of floatless carburetors: suction and diaphragm.

Suction Carburetors

In a suction carburetor (see Fig. 3-4), fuel is lifted from the fuel tank through a fuel pipe, past a needle valve, and out two discharge holes, one of which is smaller than the other. Pressure differences between the fuel tank and the carburetor throat force the fuel to flow.

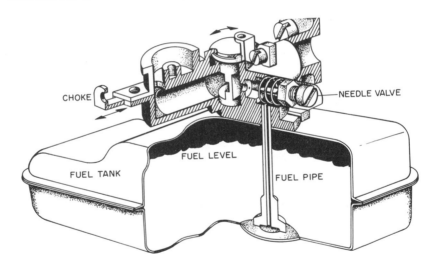

FIGURE 3-4. *A suction carburetor, the Vacu-Jet carburetor. (Courtesy of Briggs & Stratton Corp.)*

The fuel tank is exposed to atmospheric pressure by a vent in the fuel-tank filler cap. A low pressure is created at the carburetor throat by the motion of the piston during the intake stroke. A slight restriction, which helps maintain the low pressure, is placed at the choke between the air horn and carburetor throat. Also, the throttle, which sits between the two discharge holes in its closed position, is relatively thick, and in effect acts as a venturi at this point. A spiral, placed in the throat, aids acceleration and also helps keep the engine from dying when the throttle is opened suddenly.

The suction carburetor does not require an idling system, as the mixture at this speed is controlled by the throttle openings and discharge holes. At idling speeds, the leading edge of the throttle sits between the two discharge holes. A small section is milled from the throttle at this point, concentrating the flow of air past the hole and so assuring good vaporization. When the throttle is in this position, the larger hole is in a high pressure area, and no fuel will flow. The smaller hole will continue to discharge fuel; the hole size regulates the amount of fuel, which will be in proportion to the reduced air flow.

In this carburetor, the choke is a sliding plate mounted at the outer end of the carburetor. The choke is pushed in to close the air intake for starting, but is pulled out once the engine starts.

This carburetor is adjusted when the fuel tank is approximately half full, because the richness of the mixture depends somewhat on the distance the fuel must be lifted. At half full, average operating conditions exist and the adjustment will be satisfactory when the engine is run with the tank full or nearly empty.

There are several variations in suction carburetors. For example, a ball check valve may be used in the fuel pipe to assure a steady flow of fuel to the needle valve and discharge holes. Or a fuel pump may be provided to fill a constant-level container from which the fuel pipe draws fuel. This enables the carburetor to deliver a constant mixture to the engine regardless of the fuel level in the tank.

Diaphragm Carburetors

The diaphragm carburetor shown in Fig. 3-5 is typical of a number of diaphragm carburetors used in two-cycle engines. It incorporates many of the components found in float carburetors: choke and throttle valves, idle and main mixture adjustment valves, and fuel inlet valve and seat. In addition, it has an integral pump and filter. When installed, an impulse channel mates with an opening in the engine crankcase, and the pulsations of crankcase pressure are applied to the pulse chamber, making the pump diaphragm move up and down. Upward movement draws fuel into the fuel chamber; downward movement forces fuel out of the fuel chamber, through the fuel inlet supply channel and to the inlet needle and seat.

The main diaphragm is subjected to engine suction on the fuel metering side and to atmospheric pressure on the vented side. The atmospheric pressure pushes the diaphragm toward the inlet control lever, which opens the inlet needle, and fuel flows into the metering chamber and then into the mixing passages.

The vented side of the main diaphragm may be vented to the atmosphere or balanced to the choke bore. This balance offsets the enriching or choking effect of a partially dirty air cleaner.

As the engine starts, the choke is closed and the throttle is in a cracked or open position (Fig. 3-6). Several pulls on the starter may be necessary to raise the fuel pressure to the required level. As the engine is cranked, engine suction will be transmitted to the diaphragm fuel chamber through both primary and secondary idle discharge ports as well as through the main fuel discharge port, creating a low-pressure area on the fuel metering side of the main diaphragm. Atmospheric pressure on the opposite side will force the main diaphragm button to depress the inlet control lever, which overcomes the inlet tension-spring pressure, forces the inlet needle off its seat, and permits fuel to enter the inlet seat. The fuel then flows into the fuel chamber side of the main diaphragm, up through the idle and main fuel supply orifices and channels, and out the discharge ports to the engine.

At idling speeds, fuel is drawn up through the idle fuel adjustment orifice and delivered to the engine through the primary idle discharge port (Fig. 3-7). At intermediate speeds, as the throttle opening and engine speed increase, the additional fuel required is supplied to the engine at the secondary idle orifice. As the throttle opens to full throttle, the idling system fades, and fuel is drawn up through the main fuel adjustment orifice, out the main fuel discharge port, and into the air stream (Fig. 3-8).

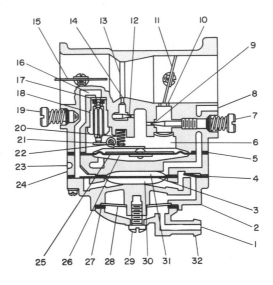

FIGURE 3-5. *Construction of a diaphragm carburetor. (1) Fuel inlet; (2) fuel pump body; (3) fuel pump diaphragm; (4) fuel pump gasket; (5) diaphragm cover gasket; (6) metering chamber; (7) idle adjustment screw; (8) impulse channel; (9) idle fuel adjustment orifice; (10) idle discharge ports; (11) throttle shutter; (12) main fuel adjustment orifice; (13) venturi; (14) main fuel discharge port; (15) choke shutter; (16) fuel inlet supply channel; (17) copper gasket; (18) inlet valve and seat; (19) main adjustment screw; (20) inlet tension spring; (21) inlet control lever; (22) fulcrum pin; (23) atmosphere vent hole; (24) diaphragm cover; (25) diaphragm; (26) atmospheric chamber; (27) strainer gasket; (28) fuel inlet screen; (29) strainer cover retaining screw; (30) fuel chamber; (31) pulse chamber; and (32) strainer cover. (Courtesy of Tillotson Manufacturing Co.)*

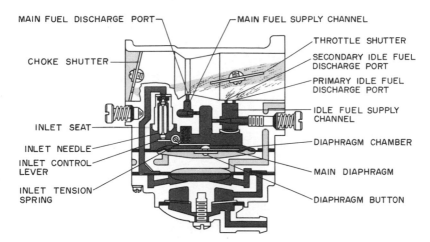

FIGURE 3-6. *Starting operation of the Tillotson carburetor. (Courtesy of Tillotson Manufacturing Co.)*

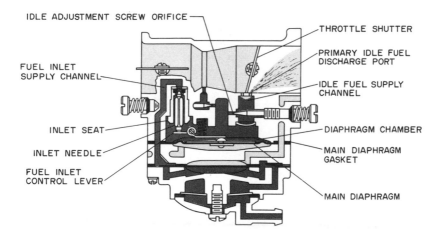

FIGURE 3-7. *Idling operation of the Tillotson carburetor. (Courtesy of Tillotson Manufacturing Co.)*

Speed Control Systems

Lawn mowers, tractors, chain saws, and many stationary engines are equipped with an automatic speed control device. This device is called a governor. All governors operate in about the same way. The throttle is set to produce the desired operating speed, and the governor maintains this speed as the engine load varies. There are two types of governors: air vane and centrifugal.

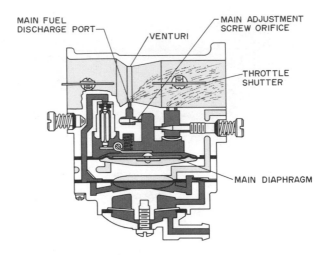

FIGURE 3-8. *High-speed operation of the Tillotson carburetor. (Courtesy of Tillotson Manufacturing Co.)*

Air Vane Governor

The air vane governor is the simplest, consisting of a sheet-metal vane pivoted within the air cooling shroud (Fig. 3-9). The vane is connected to the throttle by a control rod and linkage. Air moving through the duct deflects the vane and partially closes the throttle. The operator adjusts the engine speed by varying tension on a spring connected to the vane. This spring holds the vane so that the throttle is in its opened position. As the tension on the spring is increased, the engine speed will increase, because greater pressure is applied to the vane by the movement of the air through the shroud in order to overcome the increased tension on the spring. Generally, when the throttle control is advanced to full throttle, the spring tension is increased to the point where air pressure can no longer deflect the vane. The engine will then run at its maximum speed.

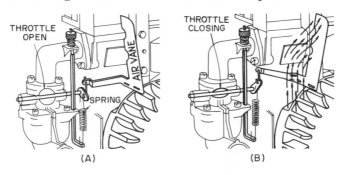

FIGURE 3-9. *Air vane governor: (A) engine not running, and (B) engine running. (Courtesy of Briggs & Stratton Corp.)*

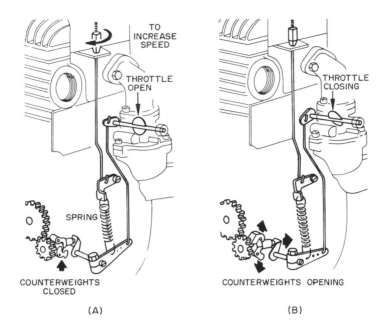

FIGURE 3-10. *Centrifugal governor: (A) counterweights closed, and (B) counterweights opening. (Courtesy of Briggs & Stratton Corp.)*

Centrifugal Governor

In the centrifugal governor, the centrifugal force of flyball weights controls the governor spring. Refer to Fig. 3-10. As the engine load increases, the engine will slow down, decreasing the centrifugal force of the flyball weights; the governor spring pulls the throttle open wide, increasing the horsepower to compensate for the increase in load, and so maintains the desired speed. If the load decreases, the engine speed increases. This increases the centrifugal force, stretching the spring and closing the throttle, which reduces the engine power.

A properly functioning governor will maintain the desired speed within fairly close limits.

CHAPTER *4*

Servicing Fuel Systems

The most common carburetor complaint is misadjustment of the mixture adjusting needles. Thus, the experienced serviceman will first attempt to correct trouble by adjustment, rather than automatically disassembling every carburetor that fails to operate properly.

Adjustment of Float and Diaphragm Carburetors

Most float and diaphragm carburetors have high- and low-speed mixture adjusting needles and an idle-speed adjusting screw. The adjusting needles are generally illustrated in the manufacturer's service manual. If the service manual is not available, compare the size of the two adjusting needles. The larger of the two is usually the high-speed, or power-adjusting, needle. The high-speed and low-speed adjusting needles are shown on a typical carburetor in Fig. 4-1.

Assuming the carburetor is completely out of adjustment, turn both mixture-adjusting needles fully clockwise. They should not be tightened more than finger-tight, for the needles may be blunted, making it difficult or impossible to obtain a proper adjustment. Next, turn both needles one and one-half turns counter-clockwise.

To adjust the high-speed needle, start the engine and allow it to warm up. Make certain the choke is fully open, and then set the high-speed needle to the position where the engine runs smoothest and fastest while the throttle is two-thirds open. (Note: Ideally this adjustment should be made with the engine under load. If this is not convenient, some manufacturers suggest opening the adjustment an additional one-eighth turn from the best no-load setting. This will assure a mixture sufficiently rich to develop full horsepower.)

To adjust the low-speed needle, close the throttle and turn the needle. As the needle is turned, the engine speed will vary. The smoothest operation will generally occur at or near the fastest idle speed.

The idle-adjusting screw should next be set for proper idle speed.

Set the idle-adjusting screw so that the throttle valve is held slightly open when in its idling position. If the engine is equipped with a governor, manually hold the throttle closed while setting the idle-adjusting screws.

When the throttle is opened quickly, the engine should now accelerate without hesitation. If the engine misses, the fuel mixture is too lean. Reset the high-speed needle to produce a slightly richer mixture, and again test for acceleration. If the engine runs unevenly without actually missing, appears sluggish, or smokes excessively at the exhaust, the mixture is too rich. Reset the high-speed needle to produce a slightly leaner mixture, and again test. After resetting the high speed needle, recheck the idle adjustment.

FIGURE 4-1. *Position of high- and low-speed needles for carburetor adjustments.*

Adjustment of Suction Carburetors

Suction-feed carburetors generally have one mixture adjustment; this should be set at normal operating speed.

To adjust a suction-feed carburetor, fill the fuel tank one-half full, and make an initial adjustment by setting the needle valve one and one-half turns from its maximum clockwise position.

With the engine running at approximately 3000 rpm, turn the needle valve clockwise until the engine starts to lose speed (lean mixture), then turn the needle slowly counter-clockwise until the engine begins to run unevenly. The resulting mixture may appear too rich, but it is correct for good performance under full load.

To complete the adjustment, hold the throttle closed, and turn the idle-speed adjustment screw until an idle speed of approximately 1750 rpm is reached.

Carburetor Cleaning and Repair

If adjustment does not correct the trouble, the carburetor should then be cleaned, and any worn or damaged parts replaced.

Carburetors generally contain fuel when they are removed, and in addition, many solvents used in cleaning are flammable. Thus, the possibility of fire exists and smoking should not be permitted in the area. The work area should be well ventilated and away from any flame or source of spark.

Before removing the carburetor from the engine, carefully note how all throttle, choke, and governor linkages are connected. Close the fuel shutoff valve, and disconnect the fuel line. Next, remove the air cleaner and then the screws or bolts which attach the carburetor to the engine.

Before disassembling the carburetor, clean the outer surface with gasoline applied with a small brush.

Repairing Float Carburetors

The float-type carburetor, shown in Fig. 4-2, has a one-piece body with a removable fuel bowl. To disassemble, remove the power adjustment needle assembly, gasket, and fuel bowl. The float, float valve, and related parts are now accessible. Remove the float shaft, float assembly, float valve, float valve seat, and gasket. Check the float for leaks by shaking it to see if it contains fuel. Floats that leak should be replaced, as soldering them is likely to change the weight and, consequently, the fuel level in the fuel bowl.

Next, remove the bowl ring gasket, the idle adjusting needle and spring assembly, the throttle valve screws, the valve, throttle shaft, and lever assembly.

Normally, on this carburetor, the main nozzle should not be removed. If the nozzle cannot be cleaned properly without removing it, it must be replaced.

Clean the carburetor body and all removed parts in solvent or a good commercial carburetor cleaner, and then blow out all passages with compressed air.

Examine all parts for wear or damage and replace where necessary. The most frequently needed parts are generally available in an overhaul assortment. New gaskets should be used each time the carburetor is disassembled.

If the main nozzle was removed, it should be replaced with a service

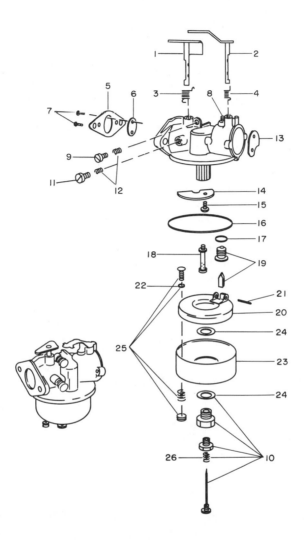

FIGURE 4-2. *Construction of a Walbro LM series carburetor. (1) Throttle shaft with lever; (2) choke shaft with lever; (3) spring: throttle return; (4) spring: choke return; (5) gasket: mounting flange; (6) throttle valve; (7) screw: throttle and choke valve; (8) spring: choke stop; (9) screw: throttle adjusting; (10) power adjusting needle assembly; (11) idle needle; (12) spring: throttle, idle adjusting; (13) choke valve; (14) baffle (optional); (15) screw: baffle; (16) gasket: bowl ring; (17) gasket: float valve seat; (18) nozzle; (19) float valve; (20) float assembly; (21) float shaft; (22) gasket: bowl drain; (23) fuel bowl and drain assembly; (24) gasket: bowl to power needle; (25) bowl drain assembly; and (26) spring: power needle. (Courtesy of Walbro Corp.)*

main nozzle. Tighten securely, preferably with a torque wrench, to a torque of 30 to 40 inch-pounds.

Install the choke shaft and valve. The valve should be installed with the part number or trademark toward the outside with the valve in a closed position.

The throttle shaft and valve should be installed next. Install the valve with the part number or trademark facing toward the mounting flange, with the valve in the closed position. The valve number must be on the idle needle side of the carburetor base. With the valve screws loose, and the throttle adjusting screw backed out, seat the valve by tapping it gently with a small screwdriver. When the valve is properly set in the closed position, tighten the retaining screws.

Install the idle adjusting needle, turning it clockwise until it is seated very lightly. Then, as a preliminary adjustment turn the needle one and one-quarter turns counter-clockwise.

Install the float valve seat, gasket, and float valve. Tighten securely, preferably with a torque wrench, to a torque of 40 to 50 inch-pounds. This assembly is carefully matched; and if any parts become separated or show signs of damage or wear, a complete, new assembly should be installed.

Install the float and float shaft, and then check the setting of the float level. When the float is in its raised, or closed, position, there should be a clearance of 5/32 in. between the outer rim of the carburetor body and the nearest part of the float at the side opposite the hinge.

Install the bowl ring gasket and then the bowl, using the fiber gaskets fitted to the bowl nut on the inner and outer side of the bowl.

Install the power adjusting needle assembly and gaskets. Back out the needle before tightening securely. Tighten to a torque of 50 to 60 inch-pounds.

Seat the power adjusting needle very lightly. For a preliminary setting, first turn the needle counterclockwise one and one-quarter turns.

Using a new flange gasket, install the carburetor on the engine; connect the throttle and governor linkages, and the fuel line. Open the fuel shut-off valve.

Start the engine and after warmup, adjust the power and idle mixture needles and set the throttle to the desired idle speed.

Repairing Suction Carburetors

The suction carburetor shown in Fig. 4-3 is assembled directly to the fuel tank and does not require an interconnecting fuel line. In cleaning or repairing, the carburetor and tank are removed from the engine as a unit.

During removal, care must be taken not to bend the governor linkage. On models equipped with a stop switch, the ground wire must be removed. After removing the carburetor, the fuel tank should be inspected for deposits of dirt or varnish and cleaned in solvent.

The throttle is removed next. The procedure will vary according to

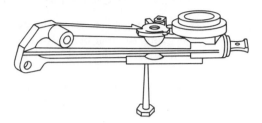

FIGURE 4-3. *A suction carburetor, the Vacu-Jet carburetor. (Courtesy of Briggs & Stratton Corp.)*

the throttle used. Old style throttles, see Fig. 4-4(A), are removed by backing off the idle-speed adjusting screw until the throttle clears the retaining lug on the carburetor body.

For new style throttles, see Fig. 4-4(B), use a Phillips screwdriver to remove the throttle-valve screw. When the valve is removed, the throttle shaft then may be lifted out.

The fuel pipe contains a check ball and a fine-mesh screen. To function properly, the screen must be clean and the check ball free. If the screen and ball cannot be satisfactorily cleaned in carburetor cleaner, the pipe must be replaced. (Important: Do not leave carburetor in cleaner longer than one-half hour.)

Nylon fuel pipes are removed and replaced with a 9/16-in. socket. Brass fuel pipes are removed by clamping the pipe in a vise and prying it out. To install brass replacement pipes, remove the throttle and place the carburetor and pipe in a vise. Press the pipe into the carburetor until it projects 2-9/32 in. to 2-5/16 in. overall from the carburetor face.

After removing the needle valve and seat, the metering holes will be accessible for cleaning.

After cleaning and replacing worn or damaged parts, assemble the carburetor in reverse order and attach it to the fuel tank. Back the throttle link into the carburetor throttle and governor lever. Raise the carburetor tank assembly into place, insert a new gasket, and fasten it to the engine with mounting screws. Adjust fuel and idle needles as described earlier.

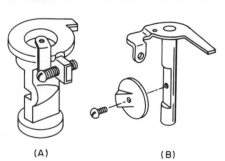

FIGURE 4-4. *Throttles: (A) old style, and (B) new style. (Courtesy of Briggs & Stratton Corp.)*

(A)   (B)

Repairing Diaphragm Carburetors

The diaphragm carburetor consists of four basic assemblies: a metering body, the main diaphragm cover plate, the fuel pump body, and the strainer cover. These assemblies as well as the individual parts are identified in Chap. 3, Fig. 3-5.

To disassemble, remove the strainer cover retaining screw, the strainer cover, the strainer cover gasket, and the strainer screen.

To remove the fuel pump body, first remove the screws attaching it to the main diaphragm cover, then the fuel pump diaphragm and gasket.

Remove the main diaphragm cover plate, and lift out the main diaphragm and main diaphragm gasket. The inlet control-lever fulcrum pin, lever, tension spring, and inlet needle can now be removed in that order.

With a thin-wall, 5/16-in. hex socket, carefully remove the inlet seat and the inlet seat gasket; next, remove the idle and main adjustment screws.

The ball-check main nozzle can be removed by tapping it with a small punch out of the body casting into the venturi.

After disassembling, clean all component parts with gasoline and blow dry with compressed air. Clean the channels in the metering body and all fuel passages by blowing compressed air through the idle and main adjusting orifices. Do not use wires or drills to clean orifices or passages as these may enlarge the openings.

All parts should be inspected for wear or damage. If either diaphragm is cracked, separated, or shows signs of deterioration, it should be replaced.

The carburetor is reassembled in reverse order from the disassembly procedure. Use a replacement ball-check nozzle. Install by pressing the nozzle into the casting with the cross holes in line with the main adjustment needle. The brass cage should be pressed flush with the metering chamber casting.

When installing "O" ring adjusting screws, lubricate with No. 30 SAE oil to prevent seizing. Packing spring adjustments do not require lubrication.

When installing the inlet seat, tighten from 25 to 35 inch-pounds. When reassembling the inlet control lever and spring, the spring should rest in the well of the metering body and locate on the dimple of the inlet control lever. Under no circumstances should the spring be stretched. The inlet control lever is properly set when flush with the floor of the diaphragm chamber.

The main diaphragm, gasket, and cover casting must be carefully fitted over the three small pins cast in the rim at the bottom of the metering body; the fuel pump diaphragm, gasket, and fuel pump body also must be fitted carefully over pins at the bottom rim of the main diaphragm cover casting. To assure a complete seal of the casting separations at both diaphragms, the fuel pump body retaining screws must be tightened evenly.

After the carburetor has been installed, make a preliminary adjustment by setting the main adjustment screw one and one-quarter turns counter-clockwise from its closed position. The idle adjustment screw should be set three-quarters of a turn counter-clockwise from its closed position.

Start the engine, and when it has reached operating temperature, make a final adjustment of the high- and low-speed mixtures, as described earlier. The idle-speed adjusting screw should then be set to approximately 1200 rpm for lawn mowers and from 2000 to 2500 rpm for chain saws.

Fuel Tanks

Fuel tanks are generally made of steel, and they are subject to rust if water is allowed to collect and remain inside. In time, the rust may penetrate the tank, causing a leak, or it may shake loose from engine vibration and be carried along with the fuel, eventually blocking small carburetor passages.

This problem can be avoided by periodically draining and refilling the fuel tank with fresh, clean fuel. If the engine is used seasonally, the tanks should be drained and flushed at least twice, once at the beginning and again at the end of the season.

To clean the fuel tank, block the fuel outlet, and remove the tank. Fill the tank one-third to one-half full with a good solvent or commercial carburetor cleaner, and drop a handful of small clean nuts or screws into the tank. Replace the filler cap. Shake the tank vigorously for a minute or so, empty it, and then flush with clean fuel.

After cleaning, one or more leaks may appear. If the leaks are small, the tank may be repaired. If the leaks are large or numerous, the tank should be replaced. Replacement tanks are available for most engines at reasonable cost.

Fuel Tank Repairs

Minor leaks in fuel tanks may be safely and satisfactorily repaired by soldering. The following safety precautions must be taken first. All traces of fuel and fuel vapor must be removed. This can be done by draining the tank and rinsing it with water or a nonflammable solvent, such as carbon tetrachloride. Also, for safety, use an electric iron rather than a torch to solder, and remove the filler cap before soldering.

To solder properly, the tank itself must be heated so that the solder will melt and flow smoothly when it contacts the tank. For most tanks, a 100-watt iron will supply sufficient heat; larger or heavier tanks will require a 150- or 200-watt iron. Use 50/50 (50 per cent lead, 50 per cent tin) acid core solder.

Clean the tank down to bright metal around the leak, using a file, sandpaper, or emery cloth. Heat the iron until it readily melts the solder, and then place the flat surface of the iron tip against the tank. Without raising the iron from the tank, test the solder against the tank. When the tank has heated sufficiently, the solder will melt and flow smoothly over the surface which is being repaired. Let the tank cool thoroughly before adding fuel to check for leaks.

Tank repairs can also be made with epoxy cement. Epoxy is a chemical compound which sets only when mixed in the correct proportions with a suitable catalyst. It bonds to practically any clean surface and is completely impervious to gasoline and commonly used solvents. Once mixed with the catalyst, epoxy cement will harden within a few hours at room temperature. At higher temperatures, it will harden much sooner. Twin tubes of epoxy and catalyst are readily available from hardware stores.

Fuel Filters

Many small-engine fuel systems include a filter to prevent dirt and moisture from entering the carburetor. Filters are either disposable or nondisposable, such as the fuel strainer, or sediment bulb, shown in Fig. 4-5. Disposable filters should be replaced periodically, as recommended by the engine manufacturer. Nondisposable sediment bulb filters should be cleaned as necessary. With this type of filter, the fuel bowl must first be removed and emptied so that the filter can be cleaned. Either gasoline or solvent can be used as cleaning agents.

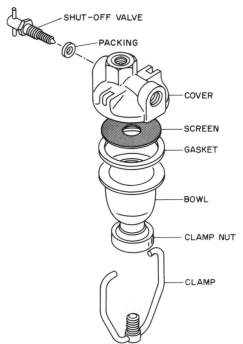

SHUT-OFF VALVE

PACKING

COVER

SCREEN

GASKET

BOWL

CLAMP NUT

CLAMP

FIGURE 4-5. *A typical fuel filter. (Courtesy of Cushman Motors, a division of Outboard Marine Corp.)*

Fuel Lines

Fuel lines are made of metal, synthetic rubber, or plastic tubing. Metal fuel lines are usually connected to the carburetor and other units in the fuel system with threaded brass fittings. See Fig. 4-6. These must be carefully installed and tightened to make certain they do not become cross-threaded or stripped. A small amount of gasket paste applied to the threads before connecting the fitting usually will assure a leakproof joint.

In many cases, exact replacement metal fuel lines are available for small engines. Whenever an exact replacement line is not available, a satisfactory replacement can be fashioned from metal tubing, which is available in a range of diameters from automotive and small-engine parts jobbers. The line must be cut to the correct length and the ends must be flared to make leakproof joints when the end fittings are connected.

Two wrenches should be used to remove and install fuel lines: one to prevent the fitting from turning and one to turn the nut which attaches the line to the fitting. This eliminates the possibility of damaging the fitting and perhaps breaking an expensive carburetor.

Synthetic rubber or plastic fuel lines do not require threaded couplings. Instead, the tubing is pushed over a tapered fitting which has a series of progressively larger annular rings. The joint will be leakproof if the tubing is in good condition and of proper diameter. Synthetic rubber and plastic tubing are readily available for replacement.

FIGURE 4-6. *Typical metal fuel-line fittings.*

Air Cleaners

A properly serviced air cleaner protects the internal parts of the engine from dust particles in the air. If the air cleaner instructions are not carefully followed, dirt and dust which should be collected in the cleaner will either be drawn into the engine and become a part of the oil film, or they will choke the engine and cause an excessively rich mixture. Either condition is detrimental to engine life. Dirt in the oil forms an abrasive mixture, which wears the moving parts instead of protecting them. No engine can stand up when this occurs. The air cleaner on every engine brought in for a checkup or repair should be examined and serviced. If the cleaner shows signs of neglect, show it to the customer before cleaning and instruct him on proper care.

There are three basic types of air cleaners in common use; oil bath, oil foam, and dry. Servicing procedures for the three are described below.

Oil Bath Air Cleaner

Remove the air cleaner and empty the old oil. Wash the cleaner in solvent and let it dry. Clean the bowl and refill with motor oil to the fill line stamped on the bowl. Remount the filter, being careful not to spill oil down through the center of the bowl into the carburetor.

Oil Foam Air Cleaner

Remove and wash the plastic foam filter in gasoline, kerosene, or a strong solution of water and household detergent. Do not use carburetor cleaner, which may attack the plastic. Squeeze dry and reoil liberally with motor oil. Squeeze again to spread oil through the filter and then reassemble.

Dry Type Air Cleaner

After removal, the dry air cleaner can be cleaned by tapping it lightly on a hard surface. Tapping too hard may deform the air cleaner. This air cleaner should be cleaned after 25 hours of operation, unless otherwise specified by the engine manufacturer. Do not immerse in cleaning solution or blow out with compressed air, and under no circumstances, oil a dry element. Replace element when damaged or excessively dirty.

CHAPTER 5

Electricity Fundamentals

A knowledge of electricity is prerequisite to the study of ignition systems and of starting, generating, and lighting equipment. The essentials of electricity are presented in this chapter, and ignition systems and other electrical equipment are covered in Chapters 6 and 7.

Magnetism and electricity are inseparably related; magnetism is responsible for the operation of electrical generators and magnetos, while the flow of electrical current always produces an accompanying magnetic field. Magnetism is discussed first, then electricity, and finally, the interrelationships between electricity and magnetism.

Magnetism

If a bar magnet is suspended so that it can turn freely, one end will point north and the other south. The end which points north is called the north pole, and the end which points south, the south pole.

If like poles of magnets are brought near each other, they will repel each other. If unlike poles of magnets are brought near each other, they will attract each other. These two facts are summed up in the law of magnetism: like poles repel and unlike poles attract.

The Magnetic Field

The area surrounding the magnet and in which its influence can be observed is called a magnetic field. To demonstrate the presence of this field, and its shape and extent, a simple experiment can be conducted. Lay a bar magnet on a flat surface, cover the magnet with a thin sheet of cardboard, and shake iron filings on the surface of the cardboard. The pattern formed by the filings will be identical to that shown in Fig. 5-1(A).

The filings will concentrate at the poles, indicating that the strength of the field is greatest at these points, while some filings will align themselves along definite lines between the poles, indicating that the field extends from one pole to another.

If the opposite poles of the two magnets are placed near each other, the pattern in Fig. 5-1(B) will result. If like poles are placed near each other, the pattern in Fig. 5-1(C) will result.

In all three instances, the magnetic force follows definite lines within the magnetic field. These lines are called "lines of magnetic force." By convention, the lines of force are assumed to leave the magnet at the north pole, enter at the south pole, and travel through the magnet to the north pole, forming closed loops.

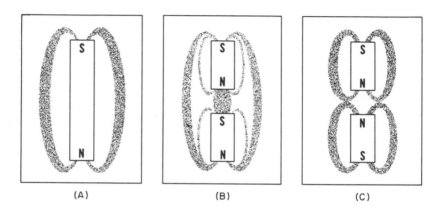

(A)   (B)   (C)

FIGURE 5-1. *The magnetic field. (A) Filings align along the lines of force going from the north to the south pole for this single bar magnet. Filings realign along new lines of force formed (B) by bringing unlike poles of two magnets together, and (C) by bringing like poles of two magnets together.*

Types of Magnets

Magnets are classified as either temporary or permanent. A temporary magnet remains a magnet only as long as a magnetizing force is applied, while a permanent magnet retains its magnetism after a magnetizing force is removed.

The principal difference between temporary and permanent magnets is in their material composition. Most temporary magnets are made of soft iron, which readily becomes magnetized when a magnetizing force is applied and almost immediately loses its magnetism when the magnetizing force is removed. Thus, soft iron is said to have low magnetic retentivity.

Hardened iron alloys, such as the various steels, have high magnetic retentivity, and have long been used for permanent magnets. However, for many years, alnico, an alloy of aluminum, nickel, and cobalt, has been the most widely used permanent magnetic material, as it will accept a much higher magnetic charge than steel will and also has extremely high magnetic retentivity.

How Magnets Are Formed

Both temporary and permanent magnets are formed by placing the material to be magnetized in a suitable magnetic field. This field may be produced either by another magnet or electrically.

Magnetic Circuits

There is no known insulator for magnetism; a magnetic field will readily pass through glass, rubber, or other materials. However, the magnetic field can be confined to a desired path by establishing a closed magnetic circuit.

Whenever soft iron or other magnetic material is placed in a magnetic field, the lines of force will alter their external routes to travel through the iron rather than through the air. This is because iron has a lower magnetic resistance, or reluctance, than air, and the lines of force will take the path of least resistance. Thus, the magnetic field can be directed where desired by providing a suitable path of soft iron from the north to the south pole. This path is called a magnetic circuit.

The principle of a closed magnetic circuit is the basis for magneto design. Here, the magnetic circuit is arranged so that a part of the circuit can be rotated; this part may be either the magnet or the iron connecting the poles. Figure 5-2 illustrates a magnetic circuit whose rotating piece is the magnet. When the magnetic circuit is closed, the lines of force travel from the north pole of the magnet, through the iron, and back to the south pole, Fig. 5-2(A). A small amount of turning still leaves the magnetic circuit intact, but the lines of force become crowded at the points of contact, Fig. 5-2(B). Further turning breaks the circuit, and the lines of force then flow through the air rather than through the iron, Fig. 5-2(C). When the magnet is turned 180°, a new and opposite circuit is established, Fig. 5-2(D). Rotation of the magnet therefore establishes an alternating magnetic field, or a complete reversal in the magnetic circuit. Using soft iron for the rotating piece establishes an intermittent field, which will vary in amplitude (strength), but will not reverse itself.

Electricity

The study of electricity begins with the atom, the smallest particle into which matter can be divided without changing its characteristic properties.

There are over one hundred different atoms which combine in various ways to make up all known substances. Substances composed of a single kind of atom are called elements, while substances made up of two or more different kinds of atoms are called compounds. Copper is an element containing only copper atoms, while water is a compound containing hydrogen and oxygen atoms.

Individual atoms are made up of still smaller particles. These particles are called neutrons, protons, and electrons. Neutrons have no electrical

charge, protons have a unit positive charge, and electrons have a unit negative charge. Neutrons and protons are tightly bound into a nucleus at the
center of the atom; the electrons revolve at fantastic speed in one or more
orbits around the nucleus.

Simple atoms have few electrons and protons while complex atoms
have more. Hydrogen atoms, for example, contain one electron and one
proton, while copper atoms contain twenty-nine electrons and twenty-nine
protons.

In some substances, all the electrons are very tightly bound to the
atomic nucleus; in other substances, some of the orbiting electrons are not
so tightly bound, and if a suitable force is applied, these electrons can be
forced out of their atoms to become what are known as free electrons.

Conductors and Insulators

Materials having many free electrons are known as electrical conductors; most metals are fairly good electrical conductors. Silver is the best
conductor known. However, copper, which is almost as good a conductor
as silver and is considerably less expensive, is the most widely used.
Materials in which the electrons are tightly bound to the nucleus are known
as electrical insulators. Glass, paper, rubber, and most plastics are good
electrical insulators.

Electric Current

Electrons obey a law of charges similar to the law of magnetic attraction and repulsion. Thus, free electrons, being negatively charged, will
move away from a negative charge and toward a positive charge. This
movement of electrons through a material constitutes an electric current.

There are two kinds of current, direct and alternating. A direct current
is one in which the direction of electron movement through a conductor
does not change, although the amount of current may vary. An alternating
current is one in which the direction of electron movement through the
conductor reverses periodically, going first in one direction and then in the
other.

The strength of a current depends on the number of electrons moving
past a given point in a set period of time. The unit of current is the ampere.
One ampere is equal to 6.28 million, million, million electrons flowing past
a given point each second.

Voltage

To make electric current flow along a conductor there must be a
difference of electric pressure between the two ends of the conductor.
Electric pressure, or electromotive force, is commonly called voltage,
because the unit of electromotive force is the volt.

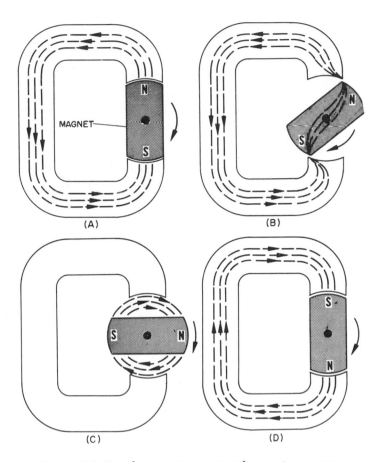

FIGURE 5-2. *Simple magnetic circuit with a rotating magnet.*

Resistance

We are all familiar with the effects of friction. For example, the quantity of water flowing through a pipe is limited by the friction of the pipe walls. Similarly, the flow of an electric current in a conductor is limited by a type of friction or opposition. The opposition to the passage of current is called electrical resistance. The unit of electrical resistance is the ohm.

Electrical resistance varies widely with different materials. Good conductors, such as silver and copper, have low resistance. In conductors of a given material, resistance varies inversely with the diameter of the conductor and directly with the length of the conductor. In other words, the larger the diameter of a wire, the lower the resistance, and the longer the wire, the higher the resistance.

Ohm's Law

There is a definite relationship between current voltage, and resistance. This relationship is described by Ohm's law. According to the principles of this law, a voltage of one volt will cause a current of one ampere to flow through a resistance of one ohm. If one of the three measurements change, at least one of the other two must change also. For example, in the above relationship, if the voltage is increased from one to two volts and the resistance is not changed, the current will increase to two amperes. However, if the voltage is increased to two volts and the resistance is increased to two ohms, the current will remain unchanged.

Ohm's law can be stated in three ways: (1) volts = amperes × ohms; (2) amperes = volts ÷ ohms; and (3) ohms = volts ÷ amperes.

Electrical Circuits

All electrical circuits contain a voltage source, a load where the useful work is done, and conductors which connect the source to the load. In small engines, the source may be a battery, a generator, or a magneto. The load may be a lamp, a starter motor, or a spark plug. The conducting path will include wire and may additionally include switches and fuses.

In any circuit, there must be a complete, continuous path for the electric current to follow. When the circuit is complete, or closed, there is continuity, and the voltage at the source forces current to flow against the resistance offered by the load. When the circuit has a break, or is open, the path is not continuous; there is no continuity and no current can flow.

Simple circuits are shown in Fig. 5-3. In Fig. 5-3(A), the source is a battery, the load is a lamp, and the two are connected by wires. In Fig.

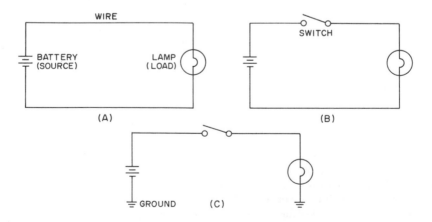

FIGURE 5-3. *Simple electrical circuits.*

5-3(B), a switch has been added so that the lamp can be turned on and off as desired. In Fig. 5-3(C), the engine and metallic frame of a vehicle have been used as one of the electrical conductors connecting the source and load. The two electrical symbols for ground indicate that the wiring is connected to the engine or the frame at these points, and the electrical path from the load back to the source is through the frame or the engine, rather than through an actual wire.

Multiple loads can be connected into a circuit in series or in parallel. A series circuit provides only one continuous path for the current to follow; a parallel circuit provides several paths, or branches, for the current to follow. In the series circuit shown in Fig. 5-4(A), two lamps are connected in a single path, and if either should burn out, the other will also fail to light. In the parallel circuit shown in Fig. 5-4(B), two lamps are connected in separate paths, and if either should burn out, the other will continue to light.

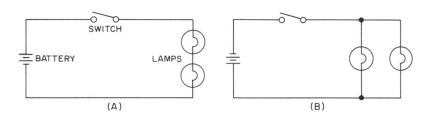

FIGURE 5-4. *Simple electrical circuits: (A) series, and (B) parallel.*

Electromagnetism

Whenever an electric current flows through a conductor, an accompanying magnetic field is produced. Thus, a magnetic field can be created around a single wire by causing an electric current to flow through the wire, and as shown in Fig. 5-5, the magnetic lines of force are concentric circles surrounding the length of the wire. The strength, or intensity, of the field depends on the current flow. Stronger currents will create stronger magnetic fields. So too will winding the wire into a coil, as shown in Fig. 5-6, for the lines of force are concentrated. A still more powerful magnetic field can be created by winding the wire on an iron core, as iron offers less resistance to the lines of force than air or other materials. The phenomenon of electromagnetism is the basis for the operation of electric motors.

When an electrical conductor is moved within a magnetic field, cutting the lines of force, a voltage is induced in the conductor, Fig. 5-7(A). If the circuit is completed, a current will flow, Fig. 5-7(B). This phenomenon is called electromagnetic induction, and is the basis for the operation of generators.

There are two kinds of electromagnetic circuits: stationary and moving. In the first, the magnet is held stationary and the conductor is moved; in the second, the conductor is held stationary and the magnet is moved. Or, both the magnet and the conductor may be held stationary, while the magnetic circuit is opened and closed. Here, the varying magnetic field induces voltage in the same way that actual relative motion between the conductor and magnet does.

Self-Inductance

A current passing through a coil produces a magnetic field surrounding the coil. When the current stops, the magnetic field collapses. In decreasing from its maximum value to zero, the magnetic field induces a voltage in each turn of the coil. If a great number of turns are used in the coil, an instantaneous voltage several times greater than the voltage of the initial source is produced. This effect is called self-inductance.

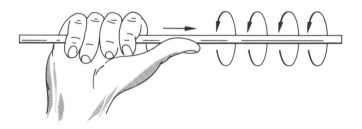

FIGURE 5-5. *Magnetic field around a wire caused by an electric current flowing through the wire.*

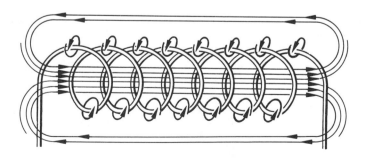

FIGURE 5-6. *The magnetic field of Fig. 5-5 can be made stronger by winding the wire into a coil.*

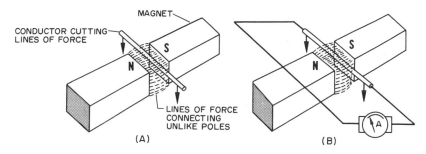

FIGURE 5-7. *(A) Electrical conductor moving within a magnetic field has a voltage induced. (B) When the circuit is completed, current flows.*

Mutual Inductance

Figure 5-8 illustrates the process of mutual inductance. Here, there are two circuits which have no direct electrical connection, but whose adjacent conductors are near each other. The circuit containing the battery and switch is called the primary circuit; the other circuit is called the secondary circuit.

When the switch in the primary circuit is closed, a magnetic field is created around the primary circuit conductors. As the lines of force expand outward, they cut the conductor in the secondary circuit, inducing a voltage. Once the magnetic field produced by the current flow in the primary has reached its maximum value, no further voltage is induced in the secondary. However, if the switch in the primary circuit is now opened, the magnetic field must collapse. As it collapses, a voltage impulse is again induced in the secondary circuit. This action, whereby a voltage is induced in one circuit by a magnetic field produced in another circuit, is called mutual inductance.

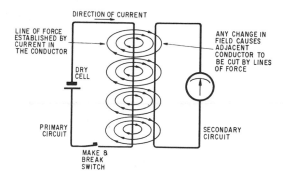

FIGURE 5-8. *Mutual inductance: a voltage is induced in one circuit by a magnetic field produced in another circuit.*

Transformers

If the conductor sections are replaced by primary and secondary windings wound on an iron core, as shown in Fig. 5-9, the mutual inductance increases greatly. Such a device is called a transformer.

When the switch is closed, the expanding magnetic field produced by the current in the primary winding induces a voltage pulse in the secondary winding. When the switch is opened, the field collapses and a voltage is again induced in the secondary. The polarity of the secondary voltage is determined by the direction of movement of the inducing magnetic field. Thus, the terminal of the secondary winding that is made positive by the expanding field will become the negative terminal of the winding when the field collapses.

When alternating current is supplied to the primary of a transformer, there is a continual building and collapsing of the magnetic field because of the continuing reversal of the current. Each time the field builds up or collapses, a voltage is induced in the secondary, resulting in a continuous series of alternating voltage pulses in the secondary.

Transformers are used principally to step voltages up or down. For example, battery and magneto ignition coils are types of transformers wherein a fairly low voltage is increased to ten or fifteen thousand volts and applied to the spark plugs.

The ratio of the turns of the primary winding to those of the secondary winding determines the ratio of the primary voltage to the secondary voltage. For example, the secondary winding has 100 times as many turns as the primary winding, the voltage induced in the secondary will be 100 times that applied to the primary winding. If the same transformer is connected so that the input voltage is supplied to the winding having the greater number of turns, the output voltage will then be 1/100 as great as the input. In all cases, the winding to which the input voltage is supplied is considered the primary.

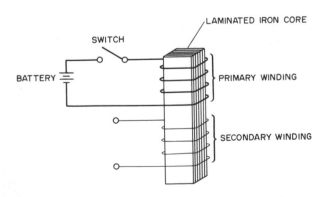

FIGURE 5-9. *A simple transformer.*

Capacitance

Capacitance is the ability of an electrical device to store energy in an electrostatic field. The electrical device which has that ability is called a capacitor. Capacitors are widely used in electrical and electronic equipment and in both battery and magneto ignition systems.

Capacitor Construction

In its simplest form, a capacitor consists of two metal plates separated by an insulator called a dielectric. Air, mica, glass, oil, and paper are insulating materials commonly used as the dielectric in capacitors.

In ignition systems, the capacitor consists of two strips of metal foil and a paper dielectric, wound together into a small cylinder, see Fig. 5-10. Generally, ignition capacitors are sealed in a metal case. One foil strip is connected internally to the case, while the other foil strip is connected to an external lead or, in some units, to a screw-type terminal mounted in one end of the case. (Note: Engine manufacturers and repairmen generally refer to capacitors as condensers, and later in the text, when ignition systems are covered, the word condenser will be used in preference to capacitor.)

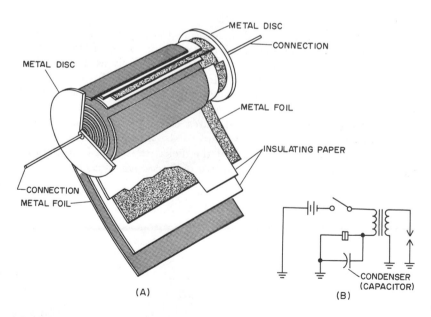

FIGURE 5-10. (A) Capacitor construction. (B) Capacitor symbol within ignition circuit.

Capacitor Operation

Suppose that a capacitor is connected in a series circuit with a battery and switch. When the switch is open, there is voltage at the battery, but none at the capacitor. When the switch is closed, electrons will leave the negative terminal of the battery and flow around to the first plate of the capacitor. The electrons cannot flow through the dielectric; however, they exert a repelling influence through the dielectric on the electrons on the second plate. This repulsion and the attraction of the positive terminal of the battery result in electron flow from the second capacitor plate to the positive battery terminal. As a result, the second plate is left with a shortage of electrons, or a net positive charge.

The charging process continues until the charge on the capacitor equals the battery voltage. When this condition is reached, there is no longer a difference of potential between the battery and capacitor; as there is nothing to force the electrons to move, the current is zero and the capacitor is fully charged.

If the charged capacitor is now disconnected from the circuit and its two terminals brought together, it will discharge; the excess electrons on one plate will flow through the terminals to the plate having an electron deficiency. Once the charges have been equalized, the capacitor is fully discharged and no further electron flow takes place.

Units of Capacitance

The unit of capacitance used to measure the ability of a capacitor to store a definite quantity of electric charge per unit electric pressure is the farad. The farad, however, is extremely large and is rarely used. The microfarad (one-millionth of a farad) is used instead. Capacitors used in ignition systems range in capacitance from roughly 0.1 to 0.5 microfarad, depending upon the design of the overall system.

Capacitance varies directly as the area of the plates and inversely as the thickness of the dielectric. Capacitance is also a function of the material used for the dielectric. For example, if the dielectric is waxed paper rather than air, the capacitance will become two or three times greater.

CHAPTER *6*

Servicing Ignition Systems

The function of ignition in small internal combustion engines is to initiate the burning of fuel mixtures within the combustion chamber at the proper time. The typical system includes (1) a source of energy or voltage (magneto or battery); (2) a timer, to coordinate the production of the spark with the rotation of the engine; (3) an induction coil; (4) a spark plug in each cylinder to provide a fixed insulated gap at which a spark is produced; and (5) in multicylinder engines, a distributor for leading a high voltage charge to the cylinders in proper sequence.

Although battery ignition is used less frequently than magneto ignition in small engines, it is used in some equipment and its operation should be understood.

The Battery Ignition Circuit

The basic battery ignition circuit, Fig. 6-1, includes everything necessary for the ignition system of a two-cycle or four-cycle single-cylinder engine. It consists of two separate series circuits. The first, or primary, circuit includes a 6- or 12-volt storage battery, the ignition switch; the primary winding of the ignition coil, the breaker points, and a condenser connected in parallel with the breaker points. The secondary circuit consists of the secondary winding of the ignition coil, the spark plug, and the connecting wiring.

Battery Ignition Operation

When the engine is stopped, the breaker points are closed and current flows through the primary winding of the ignition coil, producing a strong magnetic field. If the engine is now cranked, the breaker points will suddenly open and the magnetic field within the coil will collapse, inducing a very high voltage in the secondary winding. This high voltage impulse is fed to the spark plug, igniting the compressed fuel-air mixture in the combustion chamber.

When the breaker points open, a voltage of perhaps a hundred volts will be developed through self-inductance across the primary winding of the coil. This voltage is high enough to jump, or arc, the breaker points which leads to burning of the contact surfaces and early point failure. To prevent burning, a condenser is connected in parallel with the breaker points.

With the condenser in place, the voltage developed in the primary winding when the breaker points open is expended in charging the condenser. By minimizing burning, the condenser increases breaker point life; it also enables the magnetic field to collapse more rapidly, thereby increasing the secondary voltage.

Ignition Coils

The ignition coil consists of a primary and secondary winding wound on a soft iron core. The primary winding consists of a few hundred turns of fairly large wire, while the secondary consists of many thousands of turns of very small wire. Battery ignition coils usually are enclosed in a cylindrical metal or plastic case. See Fig. 6-2. The ends of the primary winding are connected internally to screw-type terminals brought out at one end of the case. One end of the secondary winding is connected internally to the metal case, while the other end is brought out to a well-insulated plug-in terminal. In single-cylinder engines, the spark plug lead is plugged directly into the secondary coil terminal.

Occasionally, a coil produces little or no output voltage. This may be caused by an open or short circuit in either winding, or by a short between either winding and the metal coil case. If the primary opens, no primary current can flow and no secondary voltage will be produced. If the secondary opens and only a small gap exists between the broken ends, a reduced voltage may still reach the spark plug. This reduced voltage may be sufficient to fire the mixture at moderate speed, but will be insufficient at high speed. In some cases, a short circuit will occur across one or more layers of the secondary, leaving the remainder of the winding operative. This will also reduce the available output voltage in proportion to the amount of winding that is short-circuited.

Ignition Condensers

Ignition condensers are commonly enclosed in a metal case which has a mounting bracket attached. See Fig. 6-3(C). One condenser lead is connected internally to the case, so that one connection is automatically made when the condenser is mounted. The second lead has a terminal which is connected to the breaker points by a screw and nut.

Occasionally the paper dielectric of ignition condensers will be punctured by the voltage developed in the primary winding of the ignition coil. When this happens, the two foil strips will touch, producing a short circuit. The primary current is not interrupted, but bypasses the open breaker

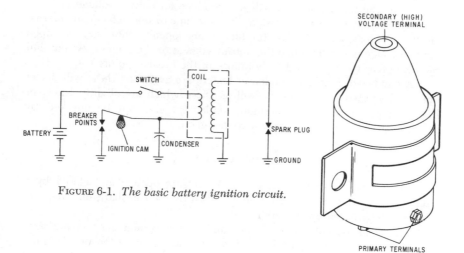

FIGURE 6-1. *The basic battery ignition circuit.*

FIGURE 6-2. *Ignition coil.*

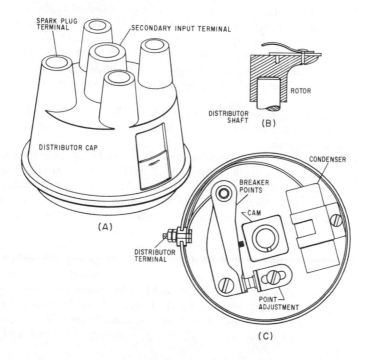

FIGURE 6-3. *Distributor: (A) cap, (B) rotor, and (C) housing.*

points and flows through the shorted condenser. With a shorted ignition condenser, the ignition system will not produce an output voltage.

Occasionally, due to corrosion or a manufacturing defect, an internal electrical connection will fail, producing an "open" condenser. An open ignition condenser will reduce the output voltage of the ignition system and produce excessive arcing and early failure of the breaker points.

A number of excellent condenser testers are available; these will detect open and shorted condensers as well as those which are slightly leaky, or have changed capacitance. Ignition condensers also can be checked by substitution of one that is known to be good.

Breaker Points

The breaker points function as a switch and are opened and closed by a cam. On four-cycle engines, the cam is driven by the camshaft; on two-cycle engines, it is driven by the crankshaft.

The breaker-point set consists of one stationary and one moving part. See Fig. 6-3(C). Each part has a contact made of tungsten or platinum. When the breaker-point set is mounted, the two contacts mate. A flat metal spring that is part of the breaker-point set holds the points tightly closed, except for the interval when they are held open by the operating cam.

The moving contact arm is pivoted on a pin attached to the stationary contact member. A fiber bushing, pressed into the pivot opening, insulates the two parts of the breaker-point set. A fiber block, attached to the moving contact arm and making mechanical contact with the cam, prevents the arm from short-circuiting to the cam. As the nose, or highest point on the cam moves under the fiber block, the points are opened and the ignition spark is produced.

The stationary contact member typically has two holes for screw-mounting. One hole is slotted so that the points can be moved to and fro in relation to the cam.

Breaker-point condition and adjustment markedly affect engine operation. If the points are badly burned, their resistance to current flow will increase greatly and the engine, if it operates at all, is likely to miss, particularly when under heavy load, for the voltage delivered to the spark plug is not sufficient to jump the electrode gap under the combustion chamber pressure produced by full-throttle operation.

If the breaker-point gap is set too wide, the dwell, or percentage of time the points are closed, will be decreased, as the points will open earlier and close later in terms of cam movement. If the dwell is too short, the magnetic field within the coil will not build to its maximum value, and the output voltage from the coil will be decreased. If the breaker-point gap is set too narrow, the condenser will not be able to prevent the primary voltage from jumping the breaker-point gap, resulting in burning and early point failure.

Replace badly worn or burned breaker points. To replace, insert points, and turn down but do not tighten the screws in the screw-mounting holes. Then crank the engine until the nose of the cam rests directly under the fiber block on the moving contact arm. To set the point gap, position the stationary arm to the gap specified by the engine manufacturer. The recommended gap varies from engine to engine, but generally lies in the range of 0.016 to 0.020 in. Use a blade-type feeler gauge to set the gap. Then tighten both screws thoroughly and recheck the gap.

Multicylinder Ignition

In a single-cylinder engine, the ignition system must produce a suitable and properly timed spark. In multicylinder engines, the ignition system not only must produce a suitable spark at the proper time, but it must send the spark to the proper cylinder at the proper time. The device used to distribute the spark is called a distributor. The distributor is commonly combined into one assembly with the driving cam, the breaker points and the capacitor.

In addition to the parts required for single-cylinder ignition, the distributor has a rotor and a distributor cap, Fig. 6-3, both of which are made of bakelite or other insulating material. The distributor cap has one terminal at its center; arranged in a circle around the center terminal, are as many terminals as the engine has cylinders. Electrodes extend from the terminals through the cap.

The rotor is installed on the end of the breaker cam and under the distributor cap. A spring-type terminal on the rotor makes sliding contact with the center electrode of the cap. The rotor electrode extends radially from the center spring contacts coming to within about 0.010 in. of contact with the circle of electrodes moulded into the cap. As it rotates, the rotor connects the center terminal of the cap to the outer terminals, one after another. The outer terminals are connected to the spark plugs so that each cylinder will fire at the proper time.

In multicylinder ignition systems, the primary circuit is identical to that of the single-cylinder ignition systems. In multicylinder ignitions, however, the high-voltage terminal of the ignition coil is connected to the center terminal of the distributor cap, while in the single-cylinder engine, the high-voltage coil terminal is connected directly to the spark plug.

In the basic single-cylinder ignition system, only one lobe is required on the operating cam. In multicylinder engines with only one set of breaker points, the cam has as many lobes as the engine has cylinders. In this way, a given lobe on the cam opens the points when the rotor is in the correct position to route a spark to a particular cylinder. In turn, the next lobe again opens the points just as the rotor moves into position to fire the cylinder.

Ignition Timing

Ideally, the burning fuel-air mixture reaches its maximum pressure as the piston reaches top center during the compression stroke. Since some time is required after ignition for the mixture to reach maximum pressure, ignition should take place as the piston nears the end of the compression stroke.

If the spark occurs too early, maximum combustion-chamber pressure will occur before the piston reaches top center. In this case, maximum power will not be developed, because power must be furnished by the engine flywheel to force the piston to top center. Also, the engine will run roughly and may even kick backward at idling or cranking speed.

If the spark occurs while the piston is traveling downward, again power will be wasted, because the explosive mixture is compressed less than it was at top center. Consequently, the explosion produced is less powerful and the explosive force will have a shorter time to react against the piston.

As engine speed increases, the piston completes each stroke in less time. On the other hand, the time required after ignition for the burning mixture to reach maximum pressure is relatively fixed. Thus, ideally, the spark should occur progressively earlier as engine speed is increased, so that maximum pressure will occur at top center throughout the range of engine operating speed.

In most small engines, ignition timing is adjusted to produce the best all-round operation within the desired range of operating speeds. In auto-

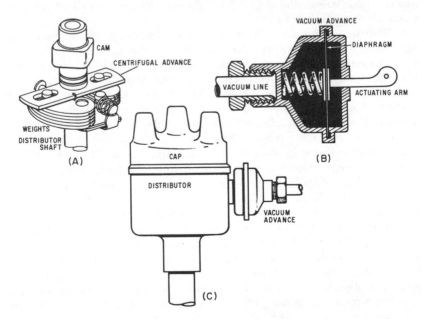

FIGURE 6-4. *Automatic spark-advance mechanisms: (A) centrifugal advance, (B) vacuum advance, and (C) distributor and vacuum advance mechanism installed.*

motive engines and in some small engines as well, an automatic spark advance mechanism is incorporated into the distributor to vary ignition timing to fit engine operating conditions. There are two basic kinds of mechanisms, centrifugal and vacuum. See Fig. 6-4.

Centrifugal devices use flyball weights to advance the operating cam as engine speed increases. Vacuum devices utilize engine pressure to advance the timing. When the throttle is suddenly opened the vacuum mechanism uses the engine manifold pressure to position a diaphragm. The diaphragm is linked to a movable plate on which the breaker points are mounted.

Magneto Ignition Systems

Like battery ignition systems, magneto ignition systems also have a two-winding ignition coil, breaker points, and an ignition condenser. Here, however, a magnet supplies the voltage rather than a battery and electro-magnetic force is used rather than electrochemical force.

The Basic Magneto

Figure 6-5 illustrates the basic operating principles of the magneto. A powerful magnet is imbedded in a nonmagnetic rotor. The rotor is positioned between two halves of a soft-iron armature. The armature halves are linked at the top by the soft-iron core of the ignition coil, forming a complete magnetic circuit.

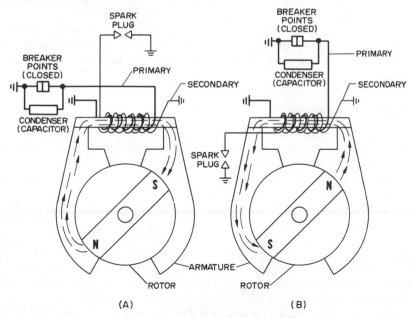

(A)   (B)

FIGURE 6-5. *Basic magneto operation.*

With the rotor positioned as shown in Fig. 6-5(A), the lines of magnetic force leave the north pole of the magnet and flow upward through the left half of the armature, to the right through the coil core, and downward through the right half of the armature, where they reenter the south pole of the rotor magnet.

With the rotor positioned as shown in Fig. 6-5(B), the direction of magnetic flow is reversed. At an intermediate point, the magnetic field through the coil core is zero. Thus, as the rotor turns, the magnetic field builds up to a maximum in one direction, falls to zero, and then builds up to a maximum in the opposite direction, and again falls to zero. This process is completed once during each turn of the rotor, thereby creating a continuously varying magnetic field within the armature and coil core.

When this varying magnetic field cuts across the conductor, a voltage is induced in the conductor. In this case, the conductor consists of a primary coil winding of several hundred turns, and the changing field generates a slight voltage in each turn of the coil. Since all the turns are in series, an alternating voltage of 100 volts or more will be induced across the entire primary winding when the breaker points are open.

With the breaker points closed, an alternating current flows in the primary ignition circuit. The closed points effectively short-circuit the ignition coil, so that the coil voltage is very low. At a moment when the primary current is high, the breaker points open and the primary voltage rises to 100 volts or more. A voltage is also induced in the secondary winding. The secondary voltage, which is proportional to the turns ratio, roughly 100 to 1, will be 10,000 volts or more. This voltage is applied to the spark plug.

The condenser functions in exactly the same way as in the battery ignition system; it keeps the breaker points from arcing, and provides a higher secondary voltage by enabling the magnetic field to collapse more rapidly.

Flywheel Magnetos

The component parts of the small engine magneto usually are assembled behind the flywheel, and this assembly is called a flywheel magneto. Two types of flywheel magnetos are shown in Fig. 6-6.

In Fig. 6-6(A), the breaker points and condenser are mounted behind the flywheel, and the points are actuated by a crankshaft-driven plunger. The magnet, embedded in the flywheel, is made of a ceramic material that develops a very powerful magnetic field in a concentrated area. The two-winding ignition coil is assembled on a laminated iron aramature and is mounted external to the flywheel so that a very slight air gap exists between its two legs and the surface of the flywheel. In this way, as the flywheel rotates, a very powerful magnetic field is directed from the flywheel up through the armature, first in one direction and then in the other.

In the engine shown in Fig. 6-6(B), the magnet is imbedded in a small-diameter rotor rather than in the flywheel. The coil, armature, and

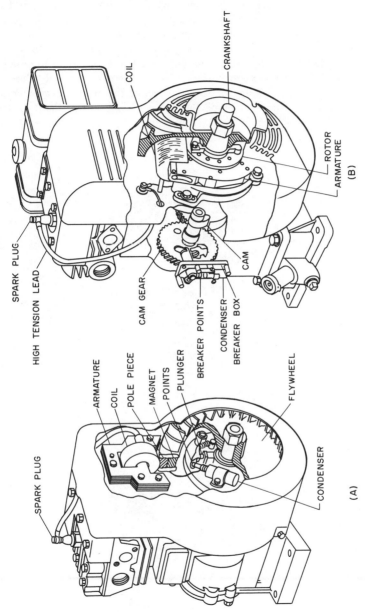

FIGURE 6-6. *Flywheel magnetos.*

rotor are mounted behind the flywheel, while the breaker points and condenser are mounted externally. In this engine, the points are actuated from the camshaft rather than from the engine crankshaft.

The flywheel magnetos discussed above are typical; however, there are many variations in the basic arrangements. For example, in the magneto shown in Fig. 6-7, the magnet is imbedded in the rim of the flywheel, but the coil is mounted internally so that the legs of the armature are arranged in proximity to the inner edge of the flywheel rim rather than the outer edge as shown in Fig. 6-6(A).

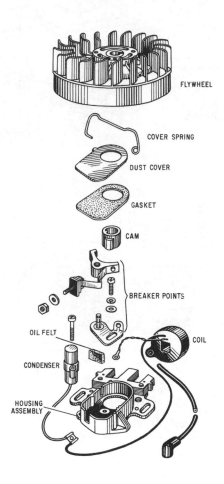

FIGURE 6-7. *Flywheel magneto with an internally mounted coil.*

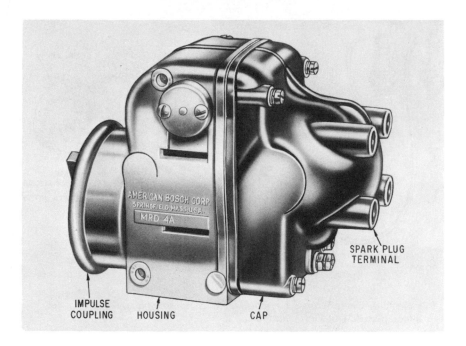

SPARK PLUG
TERMINAL

IMPULSE
COUPLING   HOUSING   CAP

FIGURE 6-8. *Typical removable magneto. (Courtesy of the American Bosch Corp.)*

Removable Magnetos

In many small engines, particularly multicylinder engines, removable magnetos are used rather than flywheel magnetos. The magnet is molded into a rotor driven by the crankshaft or the camshaft. A typical removable magneto is shown in Fig. 6-8.

When used for multicylinder ignition, the removable magneto has a distributor arrangement similar to that used in multicylinder battery ignition systems. A removable magneto suitable for use with a two cylinder engine is shown in Fig. 6-9.

Impulse Coupling

On most removable magneto installations, a mechanical device known as an impulse coupling is installed between the engine drive and the magneto proper. The primary function of the coupling is to intensify the ignition spark while the engine is being started or is operating at low speeds. A secondary function is to automatically retard the ignition spark while the engine is being started.

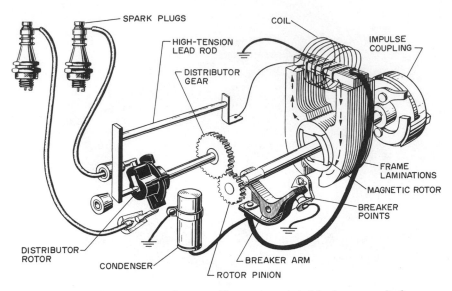

FIGURE 6-9. *Construction of removable magneto suitable for two-cylinder engines. (Courtesy of Fairbanks Morse.)*

Basically, the impulse coupling consists of a shell and a hub, connected by a clock-type spring. See Fig. 6-10. The shell is attached to a drive member that is driven by the engine, while the hub is keyed to the magneto rotor shaft. While cranking and at slow engine speeds, a pawl on the magneto half of the coupling engages a stop pin mounted on the magneto frame. See Fig. 6-11. This acts to prevent further movement of the rotor,

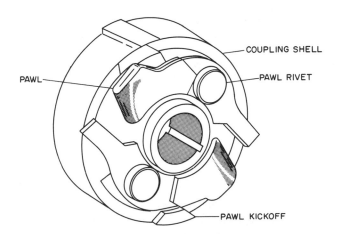

FIGURE 6-10. *An impulse coupling. (Courtesy of Fairbanks Morse.)*

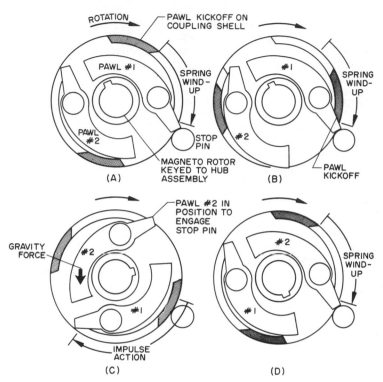

FIGURE 6-11. *Operation of an impulse coupling. (Courtesy of Fairbanks Morse.)*

while the engine half of the coupling continues to rotate; the relative change of position winds up the connecting spring. When the point is reached where a spark is desired, the pawl is released and the drive spring snaps the magneto rotor forward at high speed through its firing position. As the speed of the engine increases, centrifugal force acting on the pawls withdraws them to a position where they no longer engage the coupling stop pin; the impulse coupling then acts as a solid drive member.

Where only one spark per revolution of the magneto rotor is required, a single pawl coupling is used. This is usually the case with single-cylinder engines. To produce two sparks per revolution, a twin-pawl coupling, shown in Fig. 6-10 is used. Since the pawls are placed symmetrically on the coupling plate, each 180° of magneto rotation brings a pawl into position to engage the stop pin.

Magneto Switches

On engines equipped with magnetos, some method must be provided to kill the magneto and stop the engine.

On single-cylinder engines, a spring-type shorting strap is frequently mounted near the spark plug. To stop the engine, the free end of the strap is manually pressed against the spark plug terminal until the engine stops. In other magneto systems, a wire, brought out from the terminal, connects the breaker points, condenser, and primary coil winding to a switch. Pressing the switch short-circuits the primary ignition circuit and stops the engine.

Magneto Troubles

As in the battery ignition system, the coil, breaker points, and condenser must be in good condition if the magneto is to function properly. In addition, the breaker points must be adjusted to the correct gap. On many magnetos, the ignition points, or the plate on which they are mounted, can be shifted slightly to vary ignition timing. This adjustment must be properly made to assure correct timing and to assure that the points open as nearly as possible at the instant of maximum primary current flow. In most flywheel magnetos, when the points are positioned for correct timing, the primary current will be at or near its maximum value and a satisfactory spark will be produced.

Two other factors that affect magneto operation are the magnet strength and the air gap. In any magneto, the output voltage varies with magnet strength. If a magnet loses more than a small part of its original strength, the output voltage will be reduced noticeably. On early magnetos, this was corrected by remagnetizing the magnets. However, modern alnico and ceramic magnets retain their magnetism better than the earlier materials, so that weak magnets are now seldom the cause of low magneto output voltage. In those cases where the modern magneto magnet has lost a part of its charge, many manufacturers recommend replacing the magnet rather than attempting to remagnetize it.

In general, the air gap should be just sufficient to assure that the rotating and stationary parts do not rub. Typically, the air gap should be 0.010 to 0.020 in. On many magnetos the gap can be adjusted by first loosening the armature mounting screws.

Spark Plugs

The sole function of the spark plug is to ignite the compressed fuel-air mixture in the combustion chamber. Ignition takes place at the spark plug gap, across which the high voltage from the battery or magneto ignition coil jumps, producing a spark. A separate spark plug is required for each cylinder in the engine.

Spark Plug Construction

The major parts of a typical spark plug are identified in Fig. 6-12. As shown, the ground electrode is joined to the threaded end of the shell. The center electrode extends from the terminal through the insulator and to within a short distance of the ground electrode, thus forming the gap. The insulator is commonly made of a ceramic material resembling porcelain.

Typically, to prevent compression leakage, a circular copper gasket is placed on the threaded end before the plug is installed. However, one leading spark plug manufacturer, uses an attached gasket to simplify installation and removal. In other cases, spark plugs are designed with a tapered base which makes a leakproof seal without the necessity of a gasket.

Spark plugs are made with a number of thread diameters, which have been established as industry standards. Most common are the 14 and 18 millimeter sizes. However, 10 mm and 7/8 in.–18 thread sizes are also widely used.

Each spark plug size is available in a number of reaches. Reach is defined as the length of the shell threads which engage the engine cylinder head threads. Too long a reach may cause the plug insulator to overheat, while too short a reach may prevent the spark from occuring in the main portion of the fuel-air mixture. In the first case, preignition or early spark plug failure may result, and in the second, rough or uneven engine operation, hard starting, or missing may result. Various reaches have been adopted as industry standards. When replacing plugs, the reach recommended by the engine manufacturer should be used.

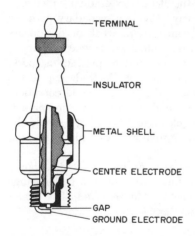

FIGURE 6-12. *Construction of a typical spark plug.*

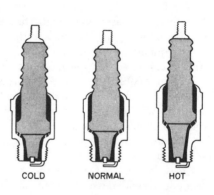

FIGURE 6-13. *Heat range variation in spark plug construction. (Courtesy of Champion Spark Plug Company.)*

Heat Range

"Heat range" refers to the thermal characteristics of the spark plug, and to its ability to transfer combustion heat from its firing end to the cylinder head of the engine.

Usually, each size of spark plug is manufactured in heat ranges varying from cold to hot, as illustrated in Fig. 6-13. A cold-running spark plug rapidly transfers heat from its firing end, and is used to avoid overheating where combustion chamber temperatures are relatively high. This condition most generally occurs at high power levels typical of racing or heavy-duty commercial engine operation.

A hot-running plug has a much lower rate of heat transfer and is used to avoid fouling where combustion chamber temperatures are relatively low. Such a requirement would exist at low-average power levels, continuous idling, or start-stop operation.

The length of insulator nose is the primary factor affecting spark plug heat range; hot plugs have relatively long insulator noses with a long heat flow path. Cold plugs have much shorter insulator nose lengths. Normal plugs have insulator nose lengths of intermediate length.

In most applications, a normal plug should be used. If an engine is operated under light loads and for short periods, a hot plug will generally operate better. And where an engine operates for long periods under heavy load, a cold plug may perform better and also have a longer life.

Spark Plug Service

During operation, deposits gradually form on the surface of the spark plug insulator; at the same time, erosion of the electrodes gradually increases the gap width. The formation of deposits may provide a secondary path for current flow so that the ignition spark becomes quite weak or disappears altogether. Increased gap width has the same effect on engine operation; the greater the gap, the greater the voltage required to produce a spark.

Frequently, a thorough cleaning and resetting the electrode gap to the engine manufacturer's specifications will restore the plugs to good condition.

Special equipment using compressed air and an abrasive compound is available for cleaning spark plugs. After cleaning, the plugs should be inspected for cracked, chipped, or broken insulators. Any plugs in poor condition should be discarded.

Before being gapped, the adjacent surfaces of the electrodes should be smoothed with a small file. The gap can be checked with a feeler gauge and may be set by bending the ground electrode as required. The center electrode should never be bent, as this may crack the insulator.

CHAPTER 7

Electrical Systems

Starting Mechanisms

Gasoline engines are started manually or electrically by turning the crank-shaft until fuel and air have been drawn into the cylinder, compressed, and then ignited. The engine delivers power and operates without further cranking.

Manual Starting

The four main types of manual starting are crank, kick, rope, and quick-release spring. Crank starting is most often used with low-speed multicylinder engines. A hand crank is inserted into a socket in the end of the crankshaft and is automatically disengaged when the engine starts.

Kick starters, widely used on motorcycles, scooters, and other small vehicles, have an operating lever with a gear segment attached. The gear segment is attached to the operating lever by a pivoting connector and drives a gear attached to the crankshaft. The segment falls away from the crank-shaft gear when the operating lever is in its down position.

Rope starters are used most widely on small engines that operate at relatively high speeds. In its simplest form, the rope starter consists of a hand-wound rope on a crankshaft pulley. See Fig. 7-1(A). When the engine is to be started, a firm, steady pull on the rope cranks the engine. When the rope has unwound, a knot at the rope end slips from a slot in the pulley and the rope falls clear.

In the more refined, rewind rope starter, the rope is permanently attached to a drum which drives the crankshaft through a ratchet. See Fig. 7-1(B). A flat spring attached to the drum is wound as the rope unwinds. When the rope has been unwound, the wound spring rewinds the rope as it is released.

Many small engines now have a quick-release windup starter because it requires less operator effort than a rope starter. The operator first winds a heavy starting spring by turning a folding crank which is permanently attached to the engine. When the spring has been fully wound, the operator presses a release button and the crankshaft rapidly turns as the spring unwinds. See Fig. 7-1(C) and (D).

Electrical Starting

Most typically, the electric starter consists of a heavy-duty electric motor, some means of connecting the motor to the engine while starting, a storage battery, and a starting switch. Both 6- and 12-volt systems are common, and a generator is usually provided for charging the battery. Sometimes the starter and generator are combined in a single unit which operates as a motor until the engine starts and then serves as a generator to charge the battery. See Fig. 7-2.

A second type of electric starter uses a 115-volt a-c motor. No battery or generator is required; an extension cord supplies power from house circuits to the starter motor when cranking the engine. This starter is suitable only for use on equipment where 115-volt a-c power is conveniently available, such as stationary engines and lawn mowers.

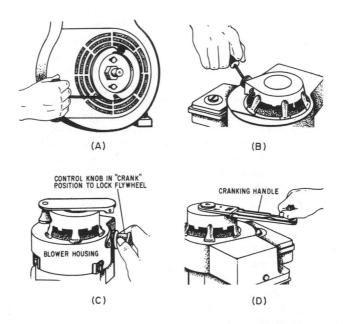

FIGURE 7-1. *Manual starters: (A) simple rope starter, (B) rewind rope starter, (C) locking the flywheel for the crank starter; (D) operating the crank starter.*

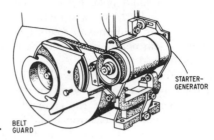

FIGURE 7-2. *The electric starter-generator.*

The Starter Circuit

The Electric Motor

Basically, an electric motor consists of an electromagnet that rotates freely in the field of a stationary magnet. See Fig. 7-3. The electromagnet, called an armature, consists of a single coil that rotates in the field of a permanent magnet. (Permanent magnets are used in very small electric motors, whereas electromagnets are used in more powerful motors, such as starters.)

The two ends of the armature are brought out and connected to two insulated segments of a rotating switch which is called a commutator. These segments make contact with two stationary brushes as the motor operates. The brushes are connected to a battery to complete the motor circuit.

When current is fed to the armature, it becomes an electromagnet whose field reacts with the fixed field of the permanent magnet. Obeying the laws of magnetic attraction and repulsion, the armature attempts to turn so that its north pole is nearest to the south pole of the field. However, before this point is reached, the commutator switches the direction of current flow through the armature. The north pole of the armature then

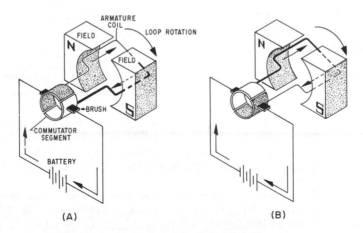

FIGURE 7-3. *Operation of the basic electric motor.*

becomes a south pole, moves on past the south pole of the field which it had been seeking, and is attracted to the north pole of the field. In this way, the armature continues to rotate the commutator, reversing the direction of armature current at just the right time to cause the armature to seek the alternate field pole.

If the simple motor should stop with its armature in a vertical position, it could not start again when current is applied because the brushes would come to rest between the commutator segments, preventing the armature from becoming an electromagnet. To overcome this deficiency and provide continuous operation of the motor, the armature consists of a number of coils, with each coil connected to separate commutator segments. Armature coils are also wound on a laminated iron rotor to increase the magnetic field and thus the power produced by the motor. See Fig. 7-4.

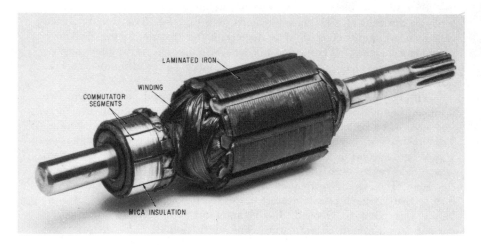

FIGURE 7-4. *A small motor armature.*

Motor Classification

Motors are classified as shunt, series, or compound, depending upon the way in which the armature and electromagnetic field are connected. The three motor types are shown in Fig. 7-5.

Shunt motors have the armature and field coils connected in parallel across the power source, Fig. 7-5(A). The field coils are wound with many turns of fine wire. Shunt motors tend to operate at a fairly constant speed, but are not suited to starting under heavy load. Thus, they are not used as starting motors.

All starting motors are series-wound or series motors. The armature and field coils are connected in series with the power source, Fig. 7-5(B). The field coils consist of relatively few turns of fairly heavy wire. The speed of series motors varies widely with the load. However, they develop their

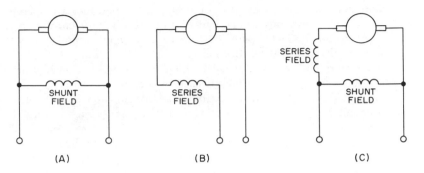

FIGURE 7-5. *Three types of motors: (A) shunt, (B) series, and (C) compound.*

maximum torque, or turning force, at low speed, making them ideal for starting motor use.

Compound motors have a series and a shunt field, and so combine the features of shunt and series motors, Fig. 7-5(C).

Series-Wound Starters

There is some variation among manufacturers in the number of field coils and brushes used in starters. In Fig. 7-6(A), a starter using a single pair of field coils and two brushes is shown (a two-pole starter), whereas the starter in Fig. 7-6(B) has four field coils and four brushes (a four-pole starter).

Both the commutator segments and the brushes are made of copper. Adjacent commutator segments are insulated from each other by mica strips. The brushes are held firmly against the commutator by heavy springs. The ends of the armature windings are usually soldered to the commutator segments.

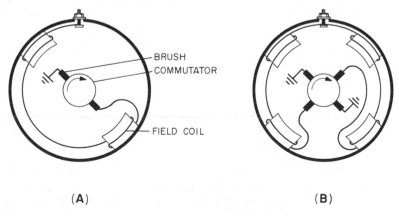

FIGURE 7-6. *(A) Two-pole and (B) four-pole starters.*

Starters draw a large current during the short period they are operated, and heavy wire must thus be used to conduct the battery current to the starter. Also, the conductor path must be kept as short as possible so the full battery voltage will reach the starter.

If the starter is operated by an ignition switch or by a pushbutton at a remote location, a solenoid switch is used to actuate the starter.

A solenoid is an electromagnet with a movable soft-iron core. A solenoid switch circuit is shown in Fig. 7-7. When the ignition switch is turned to the start position, a current flows through the coil of the solenoid. This attracts the solenoid core, closing the solenoid switch. The heavy contacts of the solenoid allow starting current to flow directly from the battery to the starter. The solenoid coil requires only a few amperes of current although the starting circuit it controls may carry a current of 200 amperes or more.

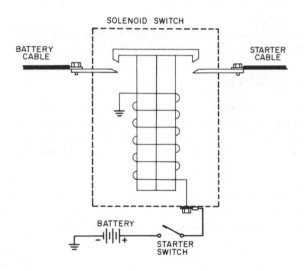

FIGURE 7-7. *Solenoid switch circuit.*

Servicing Starters

Most starter motors have a cover band which can be removed to inspect the brushes and commutator. The brushes should move freely in the brush holders, and the springs should have sufficient tension to hold them in firm contact with the commutator. If worn to less than half their original length, the brushes should be replaced.

The starter must be disassembled before the commutator can be reconditioned. Dirty commutators can be cleaned with No. 00 sandpaper. Use a flat-ended piece of wood to hold the sandpaper against the commutator while the armature is turning.

If the commutator is grooved, pitted, out of round, or if the mica insulation is high, it should be turned down on a lathe to a smooth, uniform diameter. The mica should then be undercut 1/32 in. below the surface of the commutator.

Long cranking periods can overheat the armature so that the solder in the commutator segment melts and is thrown out. Providing the armature windings are not short-circuited as a second result of overheating, the commutator connections can be resoldered. Use a soldering iron rather than a torch, and use rosin core solder. (Note: Never use acid core solder nor a separate acid flux in electrical work.)

Short circuits in armatures may be located with a test instrument called a growler. When the armature is placed in the growler and a steel strip, such as a hacksaw blade, is held above it, the blade will vibrate above the area of the armature core in which the short circuit is located. If the armature is shorted, it should either be replaced with a new one or rewound by a specialist.

Field coils are also subject to open and short circuits. Open circuits most often occur at the main starter terminal and the points where the brushes connect to the field coils. Here again, poor or broken connections can sometimes be repaired by soldering.

There is no satisfactory, easily made test for shorted field coils. If a short is suspected, the coil assembly should be replaced and the motor tested for proper operation.

Typically, the armature shaft turns in bronze bushings pressed into the starter end frames. In some cases, worn bushings can be pressed out and replaced. In other starters, the entire end frame must be replaced.

Most starter bushings are impregnated with a mixture of graphite and oil, making lubrication necessary only when the motor is torn down, at which time a few dops of light engine oil may be placed on each bushing before reassembly. No oil should reach the commutator.

Mechanical failure of the starter drive mechanism will prevent the engine from being cranked even though the starter motor operates. In this case, the starter must be removed from the engine to inspect the drive system. Individual replacement parts are available for some starter drives. In other starters, the entire drive assembly must be replaced. Most manufacturers recommend periodically lubricating the starter drive with No. 30 lubricating oil. In no case should a heavy grease be used.

Generators

A generator is a device that changes mechanical energy into electrical energy. Small engines that are equipped with electrical starters are usually equipped with a generator which produces current that is used to recharge the storage battery.

On scooters and some outboards not having electrical starters, a generator is used to supply current to lighting circuits.

Some generators used with small engines supply the direct current required for battery recharging. The electrical output of generators, which produce alternating current, must be converted to direct current before the generators can be used for charging batteries. A-c generators are known as alternators.

The alternator shown in Fig. 7-8, known as the magneto-generator, includes a series of permanent magnets imbedded in the rim of the flywheel, and an ignition coil and two generating coils assembled on the armature assembly.

In operation, the permanent magnets imbedded in the flywheel move past the poles of the soft-iron armature on which the coils are assembled. This produces an alternating magnetic field in the armature assembly; the

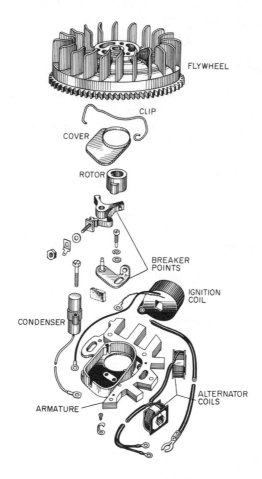

FIGURE 7-8. *Construction of a typical alternator. (Courtesy of R. E. Phelon Co., Inc.)*

field cuts the individual turns of the coils, inducing a voltage in them.

This generator produces alternating current; batteries, however, can only be charged by direct current. A separate rectifier is required to convert ac to dc before it is applied to the battery. Most frequently the generator coils are connected in series and the two end leads are brought out to the rectifier assembly.

Some outboards and small vehicles have simple lighting circuits and mechanical rather than electrical starters. Here, the electrical load is fairly low and the alternator is sometimes used without a battery to furnish current for lighting. In this type, the generating coils are tied in series and one end lead is connected to ground. The other end lead is brought out of the magneto and connected to the lighting circuits.

Rectifiers

Two types of rectifiers have been used extensively with alternators: the selenium type and the silicon diode type. As the silicon diode type is more rugged, selenium rectifiers are seldom used now except as replacements.

Some charging circuits use only two rectifiers, as with the alternator shown in Fig. 7-8. Typically, however, four separate rectifiers are connected into a bridge-type circuit, as shown in Fig. 7-9. Alternating current flows from the alternator, so that one instant the upper alternator lead is positive and the lower lead is negative. When the polarity is reversed, the lower lead is positive and the upper negative.

In operation, the rectifier converts alternating to direct current by offering very low resistance to the current passing in one direction and very high resistance to current passing in the opposite direction. In Fig. 7-9(A), current flows from the negative alternator lead to the junction of rectifiers D1 and D2. D1 is connected so that it offers a low resistance to current entering at its bottom terminal, whereas D2 is connected so that it offers a maximum resistance to current at its bottom terminal. Thus, the current flows through D1, and then encountering a reverse-connected rectifier, D3, it flows to ground and enters the negative terminal of the battery. The current leaves the positive battery terminal and flows through the forward connected rectifier, D4, to the positive alternator lead.

In Fig. 7-9(B), the alternator polarity has reversed. Current now flows from the upper alternator lead to the junction of rectifiers D3 and D4. D3 offers a low resistance to current flow in this direction, while D4 offers maximum resistance; thus, the current flows through D3 and then into ground where it again enters the negative side of the battery. The current leaves the positive battery terminal and flows through rectifier D2 to the lower alternator lead, which is now positive.

During both half-cycles, the current enters the battery at its negative terminal, as is required for charging.

Servicing Alternators

In alternators, trouble occurs far more frequently in the rectifier assembly than in the alternator itself.

In turn, rectifier failure is quite often a result of connecting the battery into the circuit with reverse polarity. Since both positive and negative ground systems are in use, care must always be taken to determine which terminal should be grounded before connecting the battery.

An ohmmeter can be used to check the condition of silicon diode and selenium rectifiers. In the forward direction, the resistance should be no more than 30 or 40 ohms, while in the reverse direction a normal reading is 100,000 ohms or more. If the results are questionable, the rectifier should be replaced.

Four separate silicon diodes are normally used in the bridge-type rectifier assembly. During replacement, care must be taken to see that they are connected properly, otherwise the rectifier will not operate and one or more individual diodes may be burned out.

Typically, selenium rectifiers are manufactured with the four rectifiers incorporated in a single assembly. In this case, if one section fails the entire assembly must be replaced.

The correct resistance of the alternator coils, if known, can also be checked with an ohmmeter. However, one coil lead must first be disconnected from the rectifier. A very high resistance reading indicates an open circuit, either in an alternator coil or in a connecting lead.

Another check that can be quickly made to determine if the alternator is producing an output is to strike the two leads together and see if a spark is produced. The engine must be operating and the alternator leads should be disconnected from the rectifier.

Defective coils or rectifier units are easily replaced.

D-C Generators

Some small engines are equipped with generators that produce direct current and need no external rectifier. These generators are generally belt-driven from a pulley on the engine crankshaft.

The inner construction is quite similar to that of a starting motor. However, in the generator, the armature and field coils are wound with more turns and with smaller wire, and they are shunt rather than series connected. D-c generators used with small engines generally have only two field coils.

Like the alternator, the operation of the d-c generator also depends upon relative motion between a magnetic field and an electrical conductor. In the alternator, the coils are stationary and the magnetic field moves; in the d-c generator, the magnetic field is stationary and an a-c voltage is induced in the coils of the armature as it turns within the field. The commutator and brushes function as a rectifier to convert the a-c voltage in the armature to d-c voltage at the brushes. This is accomplished automatically by the movement of a new pair of commutator segments into contact with the brushes each time the armature voltage starts to reverse.

Generator Cutout

Where diode rectifiers are used with an a-c alternator, the battery is automatically disconnected from the alternator when the engine is stopped, or is being operated at speeds too low for charging to take place.

Where a d-c generator is used, no external rectifier is required. Were the generator and battery directly connected, the battery would be charged whenever engine speed is sufficient to produce a voltage higher at the generator than at the battery. With the engine idling or stopped, however, the battery would discharge back through the generator. A cutout relay is used to prevent this.

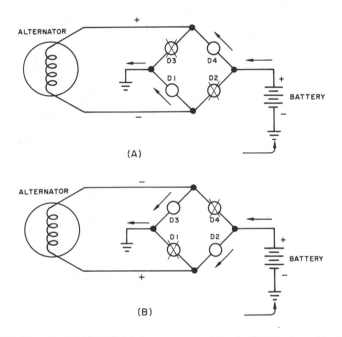

FIGURE 7-9. *Bridge-type rectifier operation.*

As shown in Fig. 7-10, the cutout relay has two coils wound on a common iron core. One coil consists of many turns of small wire connected in parallel with the generator. The other coil, of heavier wire, is connected in series with the generator output lead. The lower contact point is stationary while the upper contact is attached to the end of a flat steel armature that is hinged at the end away from the contact points. A flat spring is used to hold the contacts open.

When the generator voltage is sufficient to charge the battery, current from the generator flowing through the parallel coil produces sufficient magnetism to close the cutout relay. The charging current then flows through the heavy series winding and holds the contacts tightly closed. As the engine slows down, a point will be reached where the battery voltage is greater than that produced by the generator. At that point, the direction of current through the series coil reverses and the resulting magnetic field bucks the field produced by the parallel coil. When the two fields cancel, the contact points open, disconnecting the battery from the generator.

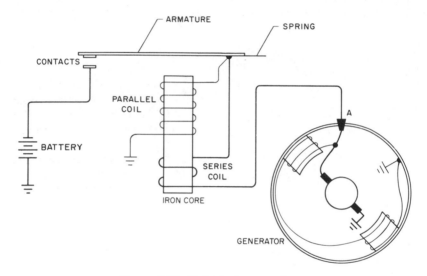

FIGURE 7-10. *Cutout relay operation.*

Voltage Regulators

In the shunt-connected d-c generator, the output voltage is proportional to the magnetic strength of the field, the number of turns in the armature winding, and the speed of rotation. If the field strength and armature turns are sufficient to produce adequate voltage at moderate speeds, the output voltage will be excessive at high speed. To overcome this difficulty a voltage regulator is used.

The voltage regulator functions by decreasing the field strength whenever a predetermined output voltage is reached. The way this is done is shown in Fig. 7-11.

At low and moderate engine speeds, the regulator contacts are closed, returning the field coils directly to ground. With the field returned directly to ground, the full voltage developed by the armature is applied across the field, producing maximum output.

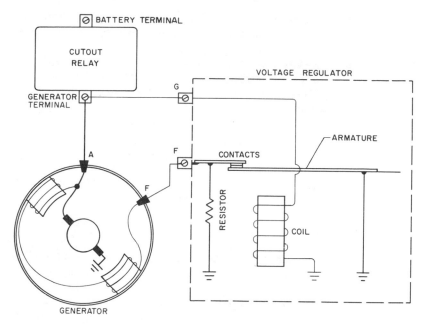

FIGURE 7-11. *Voltage regulator operation.*

The generator output voltage is applied across the magnetic coil of the regulator. As generator speed increases, a point is reached where the current through the regulator coil produces sufficient magnetism to open the contact points. The field coils are then returned to ground through the resistor, reducing the field current and the resulting magnetic field. This, in turn, reduces the generator output voltage and the battery charging rate to a safe value. Frequently, the cutout relay, the voltage regulator, and sometimes a current regulator are combined into an assembly commonly called a voltage regulator.

The current regulator operates in a manner similar to the voltage regulator. However, its coil is made of heavy wire, and it is connected in series to protect the generator from overload and possible burnout whenever a short circuit or other heavy load tends to draw more current from the generator than it can safely produce.

Servicing D-C Generators

Most of the discussion on starter service applies equally as well to the servicing of d-c generators. Brushes and commutators are inspected for the same faults, and commutators are cleaned in the same way.

Again, badly worn commutators should be taken down on a lathe, while armatures can be checked for short circuits on a growler. Rosin core solder and a soldering iron can be used to resolder the armature windings to the commutator segments.

Unlike starters, ball bearings are more frequently used in generators than bronze bushings. Such bearings can be replaced easily when worn or damaged.

Providing the armature windings, commutator, brushes, brush springs, and field coils are in good condition and properly connected, the generator should charge. If it does not, trouble exists in the cutout relay, voltage regulator, or circuit wiring.

Batteries

Engines equipped with electric starters have a storage battery as a source of electric current. The battery also supplies current to the lighting circuits, and to the ignition system, where it is used instead of a magneto.

Battery Construction

A typical engine battery consists of three or six cells connected in series and assembled into a common case. Each cell produces a voltage of approximately 2 volts when charged. Both 6- and 12-volt batteries are used, although most engine manufacturers now use 12-volt electrical systems.

Each storage cell has a negative plate group made of spongy lead and a positive plate group made of lead peroxide. See Fig. 7-12. The two plate groups are submerged in an electrolyte, a solution of sulfuric acid and water. The electrolyte is contained in a hard rubber or plastic battery case, which has a separate compartment for each cell. A common connection is brought out at the top of the cell for each of the two plate groups, while lead straps connect the individual cells in series.

The plates of the two groups are sandwiched together, one positive between two negative. Sheets of insulating material, called separators, are inserted between the plates. Separators are generally made of wood, porous rubber, or glass fiber.

Battery Operation

A storage battery produces current by chemical reaction. The chemical reaction causes an excess negative charge, and when a circuit is connected to the battery, electrons leave the negative battery terminal, flow through the circuit, and return to the positive battery terminal.

In discharging electrons, the sulfuric acid chemically combines with the plate materials to form new substances. The oxygen in the lead-peroxide positive plate combines with hydrogen from the sulfuric acid to form water. At the same time, lead in the lead peroxide plate combines with sulfur and oxygen from the acid to form lead sulfate. At the negative plate, lead also combines with sulfur and oxygen from the acid to form lead sulfate. Thus, during discharge, lead sulfate accumulates at both the positive and negative plates, and the acid solution becomes weaker and weaker. Eventually, the chemical action stops and the cell is discharged.

Storage batteries are recharged by connecting them to a *source* of d-c electricity. The direction of current flow is reversed, and also, the chemical reactions. The lead sulfate disappears from the plates as sulfuric acid is formed. When fully charged, the electrolyte will have its highest acid content; the negative plates will become spongy lead and the positive plates will again become lead peroxide.

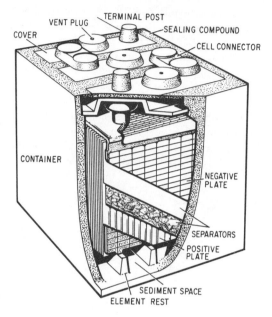

FIGURE 7-12. *Construction of a typical storage battery.*

Battery Capacity

The capacity or amount of current a cell can produce depends on the total area of the plates. Thus, for a given plate size, the greater the number of plates the greater the cell capacity.

Battery capacity also varies with temperature; at 0°F. a typical cell will produce slightly less than half as much current as at 75°F. This is because chemical reactions produce current, and chemical reactions are accelerated as temperature is increased. Thus, a given battery may be entirely adequate to crank a specific engine at summer temperatures and fail completely in winter.

Batteries are rated in terms of their ampere-hour capacity. The term, ampere-hour, is the product of the current drawn from the battery times the number of hours during which that amount of current can be drawn. For example, a 100 ampere-hour battery is capable of delivering a current of 5 amperes continuously for a period of 20 hours (5 amperes × 20 hours = 100 ampere-hours). The same battery can deliver a correspondingly greater current for a shorter period of time. A rating of 100 ampere-hours is typical of automotive batteries, while a 20 or 30 ampere-hour battery is more typical of motorcycles.

Battery Testing

An instrument called a hydrometer is used to determine the level of charge in storage batteries. See Fig. 7-13. It consists of a rubber syringe designed to draw electrolyte from the filler opening on each cell, through a rubber nozzle, into a glass tube. The tube contains a float which has a hollow glass bulb with a weight at the lower end and a thin tube with a numbered scale at the upper end. The denser the electrolyte, the higher the bulb floats. If the cell is completely discharged, the bulb will sink almost to the bottom.

The scale marked on the side of the float stem indicates the specific gravity of the electrolyte (the decimal point is left out). If the cell is fully charged, a line marked 1280 will be at the surface of the liquid. When the reading drops below 1185, the battery should be recharged.

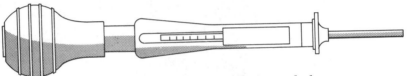

FIGURE 7-13. *The battery hydrometer.*

Battery Maintenance

Batteries should be kept clean and dry, for dampness or dirt provides a path for current to leak between the terminals. To prevent contamination of the electrolyte, the filler caps should be kept tightly in place. Keeping the battery and terminals clean prevents corrosion.

Once corrosion has started, the only way to eliminate it is to scrape the corroded surfaces clean and then remove all traces of acid film with a cloth wet with ammonia or a solution of baking soda and water. After cleaning, the metal surfaces should be coated with a film of petroleum jelly.

Battery electrolyte is a mixture of water and pure sulfuric acid. Ordinarily the only loss of electrolyte is from the loss of water. Some water is lost by evaporation, but most of the loss is due to the action of the charging current which decomposes the water and forms gases which escape through the cell vents. Acid is never lost by evaporation or decomposition. Therefore, it will not be necessary to add acid unless some electrolyte should be lost by operating the battery with the filler caps removed, or by bringing the level too high when adding water.

During operation water must be added periodically to each cell. The surface of the electrolyte should never be allowed to get below the top of the plates. Most batteries today have a fill-line indicated. Overfilling will allow electrolyte to be lost through the vents.

Only pure water should be used in batteries. If impurities such as lime, iron, etc., should get into the battery, they will either partially neutralize the acid or cause a local chemical action which eats away the active plate material. Clear rain water, water accumulated from refrigerator defrosting, and distilled water can be used safely.

CHAPTER *8*

Servicing Four-Cycle Engines

Few repairs require complete disassembly of an engine, and generally, a little prior thought will eliminate teardown beyond the point actually required to make the repair.

Detailed, well-illustrated service manuals are available from most small-engine manufacturers. Such manuals give not only the recommended disassembly procedures, but also the critical tolerances on bearings, rings, valves, and other moving parts. Reference to such manuals frequently will save the serviceman time and assure a better repair job.

Tool Requirements

The tool requirements for small-engine servicing are not great. Basic tools include: box and socket wrenches ranging in size from 7/16 to 5/8 in.; a torque wrench calibrated in inch-pounds; an assortment of screwdrivers; two or more ball peen hammers of assorted sizes; a hammer or mallet with a soft metal face; a hacksaw; an assortment of rough and fine-cut files; a bench vise having at least 4-in. jaws.

Specialized tools include a valve grinder; a valve spring compresser; a piston ring compressor; flywheel and gear pullers; an electric drill, and a propane torch.

When internal repairs are to be made, the gas tank and air-cooling shroud first must be removed to gain access to the engine itself. Frequently, the carburetor must also be removed, since on many engines it mounts directly in front of the valve-chamber access cover.

Removing and Replacing the Cylinder Head

Both valve and piston and connecting rod servicing requires the removal of the cylinder head. To remove the cylinder head, first remove the head bolts and try to lift the head from the cylinder block. If the head is stuck, carefully pry it loose with a screwdriver, applying moderate force first on one side and then on the other. After removing the head scrape all carbon from the inner surface and carefully peel away any bits of head-gasket material that may have stuck either to the head or to the block, being sure not to scratch the surface.

When the cylinder head is reassembled, a new head gasket must be installed. In no case use gasket shellac or other sealer. Run the head bolts down by hand, and then, using a torque wrench, tighten alternately until all are torqued to the manufacturer's recommended setting. Kohler, for example, suggests tightening head bolts to a torque of 200 inch-pounds. See Fig. 8-1.

FIGURE 8-1. *Tighten cylinder head bolts with a torque wrench.*

Servicing Valves

In four-cycle engines, one of the most common servicing operations is the replacement and reconditioning of valves and valve seats and their associated springs and guides. To gain access to the valves and valve seats, remove both the cylinder head and the valve chamber inspection plate.

Removing Valves

To remove the valves, lift the ends of the valve springs with either a valve-spring compressor (Fig. 8-2) or a screwdriver. The ends of the springs should be lifted sufficiently to remove the retaining locks, or keepers. See Fig. 8-3. The valves then can be lifted from the cylinder block, and the springs can be removed from the valve chamber. In some engines, the exhaust and intake valve springs are identical, and they should be marked and identified as they are removed. In other engines, the exhaust spring is heavier than the intake spring, making such identification unnecessary.

Remove all carbon and gum deposits from the valve and seat with either a knife or wire brush. Clean the valve ports and guides with a good solvent.

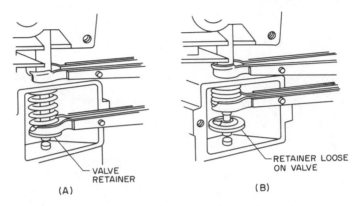

FIGURE 8-2. *Removing a valve retainer with a valve-spring compressor. (Courtesy of Briggs & Stratton.)*

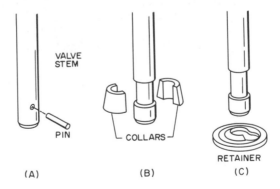

FIGURE 8-3. *Typical valve retainers. (Courtesy of Briggs & Stratton.)*

Reconditioning Valves and Valve Seats

If the valve head is warped, cracked, or badly burned or if the stem is bent or worn, the valve should be replaced. If the valve face is slightly burned or pitted or if a groove is worn in the face, the valve probably can be reconditioned.

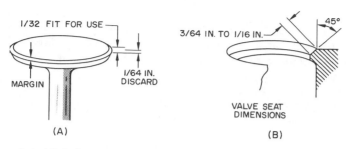

FIGURE 8-4. *(A) Valve and (B) valve seat dimensions. (Courtesy of Briggs &* *Stratton Corp.)*

Refacing should be done on a valve refacing tool. Some motorized refacing tools are fairly expensive; however, hand-operated refacing tools, which will do a satisfactory job, are available at reasonable cost. Such tools must be set to produce the valve face angle specified by the engine manufacturer. Typically, this is a 45-degree angle.

After enough material has been removed to produce a uniform, pit-free face, reinspect the valve. If the remaining margin, as shown in Fig. 8-4, is less than 1/32 in., a new valve should be used.

Repairing and Replacing Valve Guides

Before valve seats can be reconditioned, the clearance between the valve stems and guides must be checked, and, if necessary, corrected. Excessive clearance between valve stems and guides causes improper seating and burned valves. Also, when there is too much clearance, oil vapor draws up through the guide on the intake stroke, causing excessive oil consumption, fouled spark plugs, and poor low-speed performance.

Depending upon the engine, excessive clearance between valve stems and guide is corrected in one of several ways. In some engines, the guides are replaceable. To replace, drive or, preferably, press out the worn guide from the top of the cylinder block into the valve chamber; in some cases, it may be necessary to press the old guides halfway down, break off the lower portion, and then press out the remainder.

New guides are driven or pressed in from the top. If the guides are prereamed to the proper size, nothing further need be done. If the guides are not prereamed, they must be reamed to the correct size to obtain a proper fit.

In those engines that do not have replaceable guides, excessive wear is corrected in one of two ways. The valve guide is bored or reamed to a standard oversize, and the engine is fitted with valves having oversize stems. Or worn valve guides are reamed to accept a bushing which is then pressed into the oversize guide. A soft-metal driver is used to avoid peening the top end of the bushing. After installation, a bushing is finish-reamed to accept a standard size valve stem.

Valve Seats

Engine valve seats are either cut directly into the cylinder block or are separate removable parts. On engines with valve seats cut directly into the cylinder block, the valve seats should be reconditioned if they are badly worn, pitted, or grooved.

Valve seats are reconditioned with either a hand-operated valve-seat reamer or a valve-seat refacer operated by an electric hand-drill or drill press. The cutting angle of the reamer or refacer must match the face angle of the valve, which is generally 45 degrees.

Once a concentric, uniform, pit-free seat has been obtained, the seat width should be around 1/16 in., as shown in Fig. 8-4. If the seat is too narrow, heat will not be dissipated properly from the valve head and the head may warp. If the seat is too wide, carbon particles will accumulate on the valve seat, holding it open slightly and permitting the hot gases to burn away the valve face and seat. To correct the width, use a reamer or refacer of a more acute angle to cut away a portion of the face until the correct width is obtained.

On engines with replaceable valve seats, the valve seats should be replaced if they are badly burned, grooved, or pitted. Some manufacturers suggest using a hammer and chisel to break out the old valve seat. Others specify the use of a valve seat puller; see Fig. 8-5. The puller is inserted into the valve seat, and the bolt is turned with a wrench until the seat is pulled from the block.

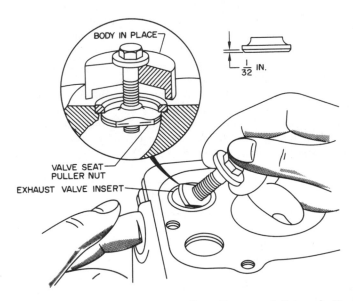

FIGURE 8-5. *Inserting the valve seat puller. (Courtesy of Briggs & Stratton Corp.)*

A valve seat pilot and driver are then used to drive the new seat into place. When the pilot is inserted into the valve guide, the driver is then used as shown in Fig. 8-6. (Note: If the replacement seats are first chilled in dry ice, they will shrink sufficiently to make insertion simple.)

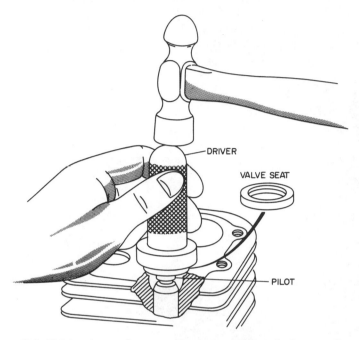

FIGURE 8-6. *Driving in a valve seat. (Courtesy of Briggs & Stratton Corp.)*

Valve Lapping

Once the valve face and seat are in good condition, grinding marks should be removed to assure a good seat. Such marks are removed with a fine lapping compound and a valve grinder. Two lapping compounds are used—one, a coarse grade for preliminary work, and the other, a fine grade for finishing. There are several kinds of valve grinders. One typical grinder resembles a handpowered drill, but produces oscillating motion rather than rotating motion. Another simple grinder consists of a suction cup that is stuck to the valve head and a round handle which is held between the palms of the hands and rotated back and forth. See Fig. 8-7.

To lap the valves, smear a small amount of the coarse compound uniformly around the valve face, being careful not to get any on the valve stem. Insert the valve into the cylinder block, and use the valve grinder to oscillate the valve back and forth against the seat while bearing down with a slight pressure. Next, raise the valve from the seat, turn a quarter turn, and repeat the lapping process. Repeat this procedure a quarter turn at a time,

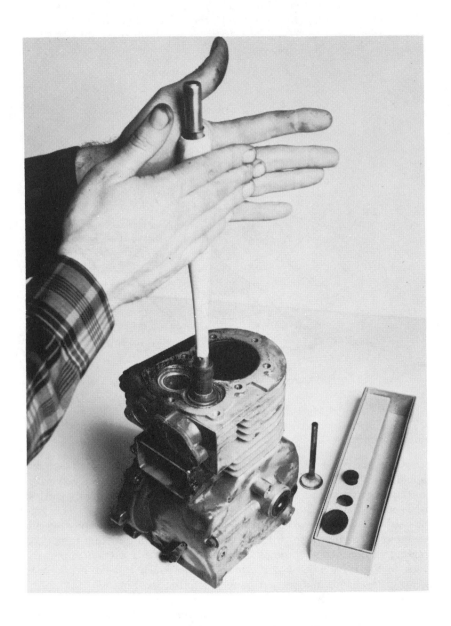

FIGURE 8-7. *Using a simple valve grinder.*

until two complete revolutions have been made. Then remove the valve and wipe both it and the seat clean. Examine to see that they are ground evenly all the way around. If not, repeat the lapping operation with the coarse compound. If so, repeat the lapping process with the fine compound. Finally, thoroughly wipe clean both the valve and seat and inspect them. A seat line should extend uniformly around both the valve and seat, and no scratches or pits should be apparent.

Tappet Clearance

Most small engines do not have adjustable valve tappets. Instead, the end of the valve stem is carefully ground a bit at a time until the proper clearance is obtained.

To check the clearance, insert the valves in their respective positions in the cylinder block and then turn the flywheel until the tappets are in their lowest positions. Check the clearance with a feeler gauge, as shown in Fig. 8-8, making sure to hold the valve against its seat.

The engine manufacturer specifies the proper tappet clearance. Wisconsin, for example, specifies a clearance of 0.008 in. for the intake tappet and 0.014 in. for the exhaust tappet, on their Models ACN and BKN. Kohler specifies a clearance of 0.006/0.008 in. for the intake and 0.015/0.017 in.

FIGURE 8-8. *Checking valve clearance with a feeler gauge.*

for the exhaust on Models K141, K161, and K181. The specifications of these two manufacturers can be considered typical.

If the clearance is too small, grind the end of the valve stem a little at a time, and remeasure. Be sure the ends are ground square and flat.

Installing Valves

Before connecting the valves, inspect the springs. Broken springs, springs that have lost tension, and springs whose ends are not square with the long axis of the spring should be replaced.

Some engines use the same type spring for intake and exhaust, while others use a heavier spring on the exhaust side. Compare springs before installing. In installation, use the compressor to compress the spring sufficiently to permit inserting the keeper, and then release the spring.

Servicing Pistons, Rings, and Rods

Generally, the piston and connecting rod are removed from four-cycle engines as an assembly when either the piston, piston rings, wrist pin, or rod must be replaced. This entails removing the cylinder head, and then opening the crankcase in order to disconnect the connecting rod from the crankshaft.

Horizontal and vertical crankshaft engines have a removable base plate, end plate, or both. In any case, the engine oil should be drained before opening the crankcase.

Removing Pistons and Connecting Rods

Remove the nuts which hold the connecting-rod cap to the connecting rod, and then carefully remove the cap. Push the piston out of the cylinder and then position the cap on the rod exactly as it was originally installed. Assembly marks are generally placed on one side of both the cap and rod to reduce the possibility of reversing the cap. (Note: Connecting-rod caps must never be interchanged between rods, as they are manufactured as matched assemblies. Interchanging them may damage the bearing or crankshaft.)

Inspecting the Cylinder

Always inspect the cylinder after the engine has been disassembled. Visual inspection will reveal any cracks, stripped bolt holes, broken fins, or scored walls. Next, measure the cylinder bore, using an inside micrometer, or telescoping gauge and micrometer. Measure at right angles, as shown in Fig. 8-9. On cast iron cylinders, Briggs & Stratton recommends reboring the cylinder if it is more than 0.003 in. oversize or 0.0015 in. out of round. On lightweight aluminum cylinders, the manufacturer recommends reboring if the cylinder is more than 0.0025 in. out of round.

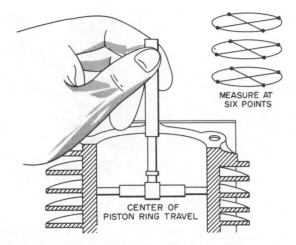

MEASURE AT
SIX POINTS

CENTER OF
PISTON RING TRAVEL

FIGURE 8-9. *Checking cylinder bore using a telescoping gauge. (Courtesy of Briggs & Stratton Corp.)*

If the cylinder is to be rebored, a new oversized piston assembly will be needed. If the cylinder is not to be rebored, the piston should be checked. Inspect for scoring and cracks, and check the skirt for wear. Next, remove the rings; clean the carbon from the top ring groove, and then place a new ring in the groove. Check the remaining space in the groove with a feeler gauge. There should be a slight clearance to prevent "freezing" of the rings in the grooves. If the clearance is greater than the maximum specified by the engine manufacturer, the piston should be replaced. The maximum specified clearance is usually around 0.005 in.

Some engines have aluminum alloy connecting rods with the aluminum itself serving as a connecting-rod bearing. In this case, if the bearing surface is scored, or if the rod end is worn so there is more than 0.001/0.002 in. clearance between the rod and crankpin, the rod should be replaced. On connecting rods of this type, do not attempt to tighten the bearing by filing the rod or cap. The wrist pin should be a reasonably snug fit in both the connecting rod and piston.

Fitting and Replacing Rings

When replacing piston rings, a slight end gap must be allowed to permit expansion as the engine heats. If the gap is too small, the ring may expand tightly against the cylinder wall, resulting in a badly scored cylinder or in damage to the engine. If the gap is excessive, the ring will leak, resulting in a loss of compression and excessive oil consumption.

Before new rings are installed on the piston, they should be inserted midway into the cylinder (one at a time), positioned squarely, and the end gap checked with a feeler gauge.

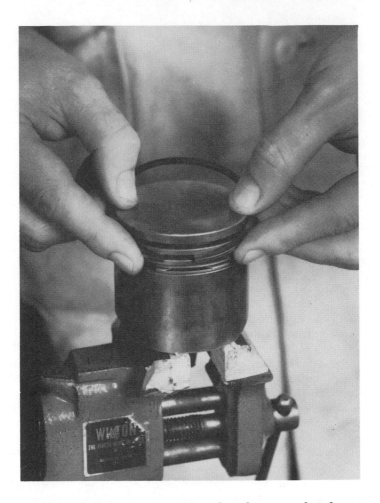

FIGURE 8-10. *Installing rings on a piston. Place the open end of the ring on the piston first.*

The desired gap varies from engine to engine. Kohler, for example, specifies an end gap of 0.007 to 0.017 in. for their engines. In any case, the manufacturer specifies the proper clearance and his instructions should be followed.

Normally, if rings of a proper size are being used, the end gap will be within the specified tolerance. If the gap is just slightly narrow, it can be increased by filing. However, this must be done with great care, making certain that both ends are filed perfectly flat. If the gap is excessive, a slightly larger ring should be used.

Once the end gap is correct, the rings should be placed on the piston. If the old piston is to be reused, the carbon must be completely removed from each ring groove. An inexpensive tool is available for this purpose; however, a broken ring, with an end filed flat, can be used effectively to remove carbon. Make certain that the proper rings are installed in each groove and that no ring is inverted.

Install rings by placing the open end of the ring on the piston first (see Fig. 8-10). Spread ring only far enough to slip over the piston and into the correct groove; otherwise, the ring may be broken or distorted. Stagger the ring gaps around the piston to minimize compression loss. Oil the rings and piston skirt.

Before inserting the piston into the cylinder, make certain that the crankpin and cylinder wall are perfectly clean. Both should then be uniformly covered with a film of oil, which will aid insertion and assure instant lubrication when the engine is started.

Make certain that the connecting rod is positioned squarely with the crankpin and is in its original position.

Use a ring compressor to compress the rings so that the piston can be inserted into the cylinder. See Fig. 8-11. Tighten the compressor slightly and then, after checking to see that it is positioned squarely on the piston, tighten the compressor to fully compress the rings and then loosen slightly. Insert the lower portion of the piston skirt, until the ring compressor rests squarely against the top surface of the cylinder block. A hammer handle can be used to drive the piston from the compressor into the cylinder. Once the upper ring has entered the cylinder, grasp the connecting rod and guide it so that the rod bearing mates squarely with the crankpin.

Replace the cap on the connecting rod, making certain to match the assembly marks on the rod and cap. Replace the connecting-rod nuts or cap screws, as well as the oil dipper, if used. Rod nuts or screws should be tightened uniformly to the torque recommended by the manufacturer.

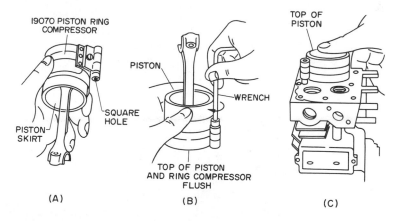

FIGURE 8-11. *Installing a piston assembly. (Courtesy of Briggs & Stratton Corp.)*

(Note: Some type of locking device is always used with connecting-rod screws and nuts. The device may be cotter keys, self-locking nuts, or a locking plate with tabs that are bent against the nut sides after they are tightened. For safety, a new locking device of the proper type should be used each time an engine is torn down and reassembled.)

The cylinder head and base plate should now be replaced, using new gaskets at each location. The shroud, gas tank, and any other parts removed should then be replaced.

After filling the crankcase with new oil of the proper viscosity, start the engine, allow it to operate at moderate speed and without load for at least an hour. As the engine operates, watch for oil leaks and listen for any unusal noises. Full load should not be applied to the engine until it has had at least five hours of break in time.

Servicing Shafts, Bearings, and Seals

A number of repair operations not involving the piston or valve system are sometimes required in servicing four-cycle engines. Some of the more common repairs of this nature involve the replacement of the connecting-rod and main bearing, the oil seal, the crankshaft, and less frequently, the camshaft and timing gear. The disassembly and reassembly procedures required for the more common repairs of this type are covered in this section.

Connecting-Rod Bearing

Where precision-insert connecting-rod bearings are used, the rod bearing can be replaced without removing the rod and piston from the cylinder. The cast iron Cushman engine is typical of this kind of construction.

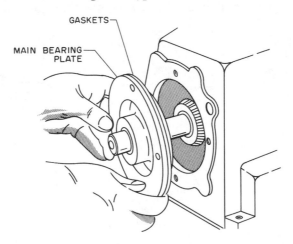

FIGURE 8-12. *Removing the main bearing plate. (Courtesy of Wisconsin Motor Corp.)*

To replace the connecting-rod bearing on this kind of engine, first drain the oil, then remove the base plate from the engine. Turn the crankshaft until the nuts holding the bearing cap to the rod are accessible. Remove the four self-locking nuts and the cap, and then push the connecting rod away from the crankpin.

Inspect the crankpin for pits and scoring. If the surface appears smooth, check the diameter with a micrometer. If the crankpin is out of round 0.001 in. or more or is flat on one side, the crankshaft should be removed and ground for undersize bearings. In addition to standard size bearings, 0.005, 0.010 and 0.020 in., undersize insert bearings are supplied for use with reground crankshafts.

Carefully pry the old bearing inserts from the rod and cap. Place one of the new bearing inserts in the rod and the other in the cap. Make certain the locking tabs are positioned properly, then seat the two inserts. Oil the bearing surfaces and pull the connecting rod down so that the bearing mates with the crankpin.

Replace the bearing cap so that the locating punch mark on the cap is in line with the one on the rod. When the self-locking connecting-rod nuts are tight, a slight amount of drag should be felt as the crankshaft is turned. There should also be a slight amount of end play. If the bearing is too tight it will burn out.

Crankshafts

To illustrate crankshaft removal, the procedure recommended by the Wisconsin Motor Corp. for their Models ACN and BKN will be described.

First remove the rope starter sheave. This can be done by hitting a sharp blow against the handle of a wrench, fitted to the hexagon hub of the sheave, in a counter-clockwise direction.

Next, remove the flywheel. The flywheel is mounted to a taper on the crankshaft. To remove, take a firm hold on the flywheel, pull outward, and at the same time, strike squarely on the end of the crankshaft with a babbit hammer. The flywheel should now slide off the taper of the crankshaft. Do not use a hard hammer as it may ruin the crankshaft and bearings. Later, when reassembling the flywheel be sure the Woodruff key is in position on the shaft and that the keyway is lined up accurately with the key.

Next, remove the engine base and disconnect the connecting rod from the crankpin. Push the rod up into the cylinder so that it will not interfere with the crankshaft during removal.

Last, remove the four bolts in the main bearing plate at the take-off end of the engine. The bearing plate can then be pried off and the crankshaft removed from this end of the crankcase. Be sure to keep gaskets in place (Fig. 8-12). These gaskets are used to give the proper end play to the tapered roller main bearings on the crankshaft. This end play should be 0.002 to 0.004 in. when the engine is cold. There is practically no wear in the roller bearings so that readjustment is seldom necessary when properly assembled.

FIGURE 8-13. *Crankshaft with scored crankpin.*

With the crankshaft removed, it can be inspected for wear and damage. If warped, it should be replaced. If bearing surfaces are in bad condition, the shaft can be reground and fitted with undersize bearings. See Fig. 8-13.

When reassembling the crankshaft, the timing marks on the crankshaft gear and the camshaft gear must be matched, as shown in Fig. 8-14, or

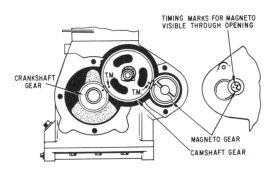

FIGURE 8-14. *Aligning timing marks. (Courtesy of Wisconsin Motor Corp.)*

the engine will not operate properly. If timing is off considerably, the engine will not run at all.

Tighten main bearing plate capscrews to a torque of 14 to 18 foot-pounds.

Main Bearings

Many different types of main bearings are used with small engines: tapered roller main bearings, ball bearings, and most frequently, plain bearings, or bushings. Regardless of the main bearing type, once the crankshaft has been removed, the main bearings can be inspected and measured for wear. Bearings are removed and replaced with a press, used as shown in Fig. 8-15.

When pressing in a new bushing, care must be taken to align the oil hole in the bushing with the oil hole in the crankcase. Bushings must then be reamed to the proper diameter.

Replacing Oil Seals

To prevent oil leaks, a seal is used at both main bearings. If not already worn, oil seals are frequently damaged during crankshaft removal. Therefore, whenever the shaft is replaced, the oil seals also should be replaced.

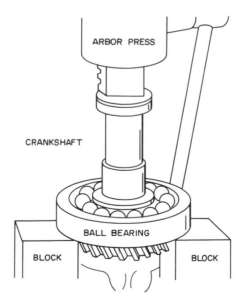

FIGURE 8-15. *Remove main bearings. (Courtesy of Briggs & Stratton Corp.)*

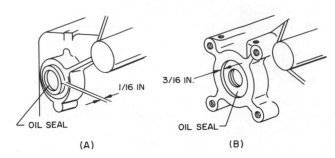

FIGURE 8-16. *Positioning oil seals. (Courtesy of Briggs & Stratton Corp.)*

In Briggs & Stratton engines, the oil seal is assembled with the sharp edge of the leather or rubber toward the inside of the engine. Most Briggs & Stratton oil seals should be pushed in flush with the hub; however, on models N, 6, 8, 55, and 65, which have plain bearings, the oil seal should protrude 1/16 in. as shown in Fig. 8-16(A). Where ball bearings are used in the same engines, the seal should be pushed into the hub about 3/16 in. as shown at Fig. 8-16(B).

CHAPTER *9*

Servicing Two-Cycle Engines

Most two-cycle engines have a higher horsepower-to-weight ratio than four-cycle engines. To a certain extent this is because die cast aluminum parts are used in their construction. Such parts are relatively fragile and must be handled carefully so that they are not broken and so that threads are not stripped during assembly.

Neither timing gears, camshaft, nor poppet valves are used in two-cycle engines. Thus, some sources of trouble are eliminated. However, the cylinder ports, which correspond to four-cycle engine valves, accumulate carbon, which must be removed periodically or the port will become blocked, drastically reducing engine performance.

Most two-cycle engines have a reed-type inlet valve which admits the fuel-air mixture into the crankcase. A defective reed valve can cause hard starting and poor performance. If the reed is broken or otherwise fails to close, the engine may not start at all. Generally the carburetor must first be removed to gain access to the reed valve for inspection or replacement.

Servicing Pistons, Rings, and Cylinders

In most air-cooled two-cycle engines the cylinder is removable from the crankcase. This simplifies the replacement of piston rings, as well as the replacement of the cylinder and piston. A typical two-cycle engine, the Canadien chain saw, is used to illustrate how this kind of engine is disassembled for repair and servicing. An exploded view of the engine appears in Fig. 9-1.

Preliminary Disassembly

To disassemble the engine, first remove the outer and inner shrouds and the front handle.

Next remove the carburetor. To do so, disconnect the fuel line at the carburetor, and then remove the air filter. After removing two hex nuts, move the carburetor back and up until the throttle link comes clear of the hook on the throttle lever. The carburetor will then be free.

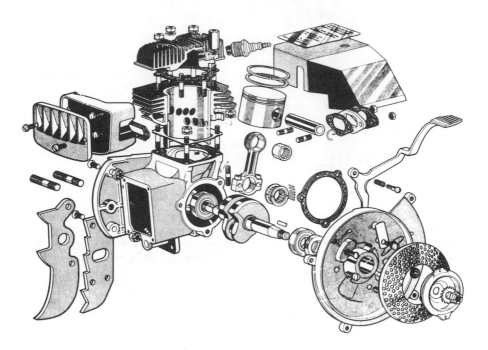

FIGURE 9-1. *Exploded view of Canadien Engine. (Courtesy of Power Machinery, a division of Bristol Aero Industries Ltd.)*

Removing the Cylinder Head

To remove the cylinder head, first remove the exhaust manifold cover and then remove the upper main body screw from the manifold. (Note: this screw screws into the cylinder head.) Remove the cylinder-head hex nuts, noting the position of the special, long shroud nut. Place a screwdriver between the head and the cylinder block fins, gently prying at intervals around the head to break the head-block gasket seal. Then place two screwdrivers at opposite sides of the head and carefully pry it upward until free.

Removing the Cylinder Block

Use a 7/16-in. open-end wrench to loosen the cylinder base mounting nuts. Then tap the cylinder block gently upward with a fiber hammer or wooden block to break the cylinder block-crankcase gasket seal. See Fig. 9-2. Remove the cylinder base nuts, and then lift the cylinder block away from the crankcase and piston.

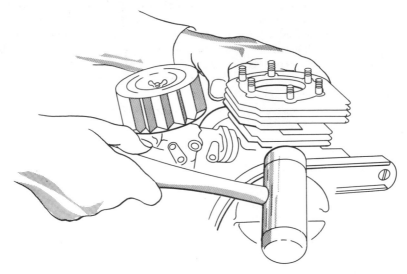

FIGURE 9-2. *Removing the cylinder block. (Courtesy of Power Machinery, a division of Bristol Aero Industries Ltd.)*

Cleaning and Inspecting

Remove the piston rings and thoroughly clean all parts. A knife can be used to remove carbon from the piston head and inner surface of the cylinder head and a wooden stick used to remove any carbon accumulated in the cylinder ports. Use a piston groove cleaner to remove all carbon from the piston ring grooves. If a groove cleaner is not available, an old ring can be broken and the end filed flat for this purpose.

After removing all carbon, wash the cylinder and head in solvent and clean the piston with a solvent-saturated rag.

All parts should now be inspected. Check the head for cracks, and the machined surface for warpage and burned areas. Inspect the cylinder bore for excessive wear or scoring. (Note: Aluminum cylinders with plated bores are widely used in two-cycle engines. If the plating is worn through so as to expose the soft aluminum, the cylinder must be replaced.)

Removing the Piston

If the piston is scored or so worn that it no longer fits the cylinder snugly or if the wrist-pin bearing is damaged or worn, the piston must be removed from the connecting rod, and the worn or damaged parts replaced. Check the wrist-pin bearing by moving the piston in relation to the connecting rod. If the play is excessive, the wrist-pin, bearing, or both, must be replaced.

Remove the wrist-pin retainer clips with needle pliers. Heat the piston head on both sides around the wrist-pin holes, using a propane torch, as shown in Fig. 9-3. This will expand the piston openings sufficiently to push the pin from the piston. A special tool is used for this. See Fig. 9-4. To prevent bending the connecting rod, hold the heated piston in one hand (use an asbestos glove or rag) while removing the pin with the tool.

The piston, wrist pin, or wrist-pin bearing can now be replaced. The piston should be heated again. The opposite end of the tool used to remove the pin can be used to insert a new wrist pin.

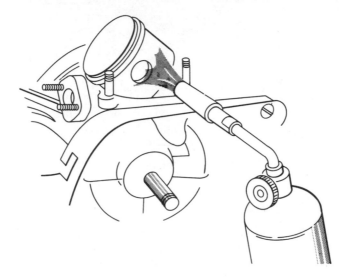

FIGURE 9-3. *Heating the piston with a propane torch. (Courtesy of Power Machinery, a division of Bristol Aero Industries Ltd.)*

Replacing Piston Rings

Once the cylinder and piston are in good condition, new piston rings should be installed. Care must be taken to assure that the proper ring is placed in each groove and that no ring is inverted, top to bottom. (Note: In many instances, the two or three rings used in two-cycle engines are identical and can be installed in any position.) The ring gaps should be staggered around the piston.

The cylinder wall, piston skirt, and rings should be thoroughly oiled before the cylinder is replaced. As with four-cycle engines, a ring compressor should be used to install the piston in the cylinder.

Reassembly

In general, reassembly is the reverse of the disassembly procedure. In all cases, new gaskets should be used, and all nuts and bolts should be carefully and uniformly tightened to the manufacturer' specified torque. For example, Canadien recommends a torque of 75 inch-pounds for both the cylinder-head nuts and the cylinder-base mounting nuts. This torque is typical for engines of this type.

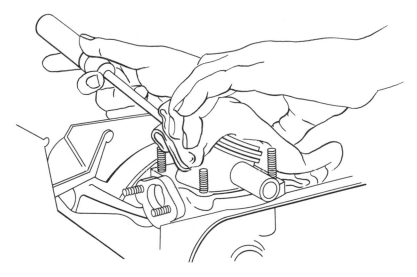

FIGURE 9-4. *Removing the wrist pin. (Courtesy of Power Machinery, a division of Bristol Aero Industries Ltd.)*

Servicing Connecting Rods and Bearings

If the connecting rod is bent or broken or the connecting-rod bearing is worn, replacement is necessary. On Canadien engines, the connecting rod can be removed through the cylinder opening in the crankcase. A special tool, used to support the connecting rod cap while removing the rod, is available from the manufacturer.

Loosen the two connecting-rod screws with a 5/32-in. allen wrench. Place the cap support tool under the cap, finish removing the screws, as shown in Fig. 9-5, and lift out the rod, complete with the top half of the bearing cage, and the six top-half roller bearings.

Rotate the crankshaft to permit removal of the cap, the lower half of the bearing cage, and six lower-half roller bearings. Make certain that all twelve rollers are removed and not lost in the crankcase.

The connecting rod, bearings, or both can now be replaced, providing the crankshaft is in good condition. In reassembly, the punch marks on the side of the rod and cap should be together and to the back of the engine. One side of each section of the bearing cage is notched at the divide. The notched rim should be aligned with the punch marks on the rod and cap, and to the back of the engine. The connecting-rod screws should be tightened to a torque of 55 inch-pounds.

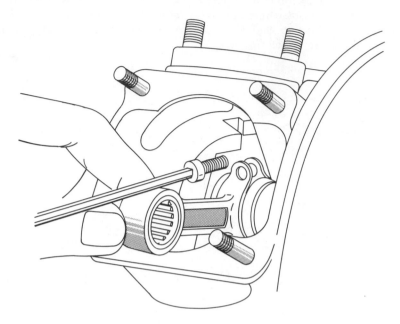

FIGURE 9-5. *Removing connecting-rod screws. (Courtesy of Power Machinery, a division of Bristol Aero Industries Ltd.)*

Servicing Crankshafts, Main Bearings, and Seals

To replace the crankshaft, main bearings, or crankcase seals, the Canadien engine must be completely disassembled. The cylinder block and connecting rod are disassembled as described earlier. The crankcase is then taken apart as follows.

Remove the cooling shroud and rewind starter as an assembly, and then remove the nut holding the flywheel to the crankshaft. Since this nut has a left-hand thread, it is loosened in a clockwise direction, with an impact wrench, if available. Otherwise, lock the flywheel by inserting a screwdriver at the base of a blower fin and holding it firmly against some stationary part of the engine, and then remove the flywheel nut with an ordinary socket wrench. (Note: Make certain that the screwdriver extends fully to the base of the fin. Otherwise the fin may break off, leaving the flywheel unbalanced; in which case it must be replaced.)

Remove the flywheel nut washer, and then pull free the starter cup and screen. Next, attach the combination clutch-and-flywheel puller, available from the manufacturer, to the three cap screws inserted in the threaded holes in the flywheel and tighten the center bolt against the end of the crankshaft (Fig. 9-6). If necessary, the center bolt can be tapped sharply to free the flywheel. Remove the flywheel from the crankshaft.

Note the position of the timing mark opposite the top magneto stator mounting boss. (See Fig. 9-7.) If the stator is to be replaced, the punch mark on the stator should be lined up with the timing mark. If a new stator is to be used, it should be positioned relative to the stator being replaced.

Remove the two screws holding the magneto stator, then remove the cover from the breaker-point box and the magneto cam. Disconnect the stop-switch wire from the stator and slide the stator assembly over the end of the crankshaft.

Removing the Clutch

Next, remove the clutch. The clutch is located on the end of the crankshaft opposite to the flywheel and can be removed with the same puller used to remove the flywheel.

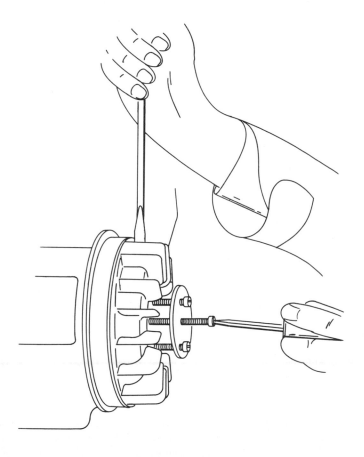

FIGURE 9-6. *Removing the flywheel. (Courtesy of Power Machinery, a division of Bristol Aero Industries Ltd.)*

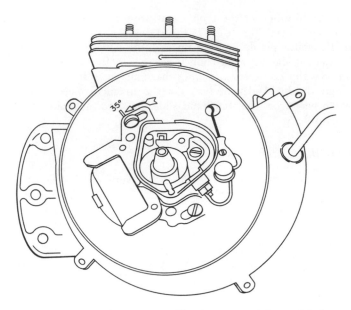

FIGURE 9-7. *Magneto and stator assembly. (Courtesy of Power Machinery, a division of Bristol Aero Industries Ltd.)*

Removing the Crankshaft

Remove the three screws from the stator backing plate, and then, with a propane torch, heat the crankcase around the clutch-side main bearing. (Ideally, a uniform temperature just under 212°F.)

Hold the crankcase in one hand, as shown in Fig. 9-8, and strike squarely on the end of the crankshaft with a soft-nosed hammer until the shaft and plate drop away.

Use the torch to heat around the main bearing in the backing plate, and then drive the crankshaft free. The main bearings can now be removed from the crankshaft, with a standard bearing puller. The crankcase seals can be removed with a seal driver, available from the engine manufacturer.

Reassembly

Reassembly should be in reverse order to the disassembly procedures given, with any worn or damaged parts replaced and all new crankcase seals installed.

Main bearings are installed more easily if they first are heated in a can of hot oil. If the crankshaft is supported in a vise, the bearings may be driven in place with a hammer and a piece of metal tubing of proper diameter to bear against the inner-bearing race.

Heat the stator backing plate to just under 212°F., then insert the bearing seal, preferably using a suitable driver and an oil-seal protector sleeve. Seals should be inserted 1/16 in. below the surface of the casting.

Again heat the stator backing plate and then insert the crankshaft with the bearing into the plate. Allow the stator plate to cool before continuing with the assembly.

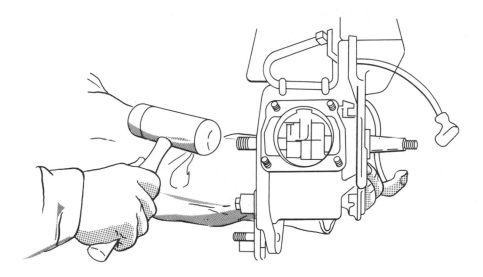

FIGURE 9-8. *Removing the stator backing plate. (Courtesy of Power Machinery, a division of Bristol Aero Industries Ltd.)*

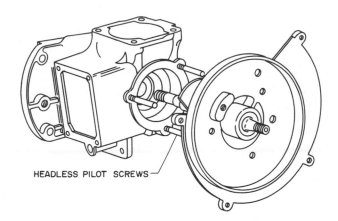

HEADLESS PILOT SCREWS

FIGURE 9-9. *Assembly of stator backing plate and crankshaft to crankcase. (Courtesy of Power Machinery, a division of Bristol Aero Industries Ltd.)*

Install the headless pilot screws in the crankcase, as shown in Fig. 9-9, and use a new backing-plate gasket over the pilot screws. Heat the crankcase and then insert the crankshaft through to the clutch side of the engine, piloting the stator backing plate over the pilot screws. Quickly press the backing plate and crankcase firmly together. Remove the pilot screws and replace with the original screws. Finally, install the remaining crankcase seal.

Engine assembly should now be completed, and all nuts tightened to the manufacturer's recommended torque.

CHAPTER *10*

Servicing Outboard Motors

Outboard motors are typically two-cycle, water-cooled engines. They may use from one to six cylinders, and the rated horsepower ranges from less than two to more than eighty.

For discussion and service purposes, the outboard may be divided into an upper and a lower assembly. The upper assembly contains the motor proper, or the powerhead, as it is generally called. The lower assembly contains the drive system, water pump, and exhaust line. A typical outboard motor appears in Fig. 10-1.

The cylinders are positioned horizontally, in either a V or inline arrangement. The crankshaft is mounted vertically and attached to a driveshaft fitted with a pinion gear at its lower end. The pinion gear is meshed with a gear attached to the propeller shaft. In all but the smallest outboards, two propeller shaft gears are used. This permits forward and reverse operation, as well as a neutral position.

Typical Powerhead

An exploded view of a typical outboard powerhead is shown in Fig. 10-2. This motor, rated at 9½ hp., is water-cooled and has two two-cycle cylinders in an inline arrangement.

The two cylinders are cast in a common block. The crankcase is removable. Needle bearings are used for the main and connecting-rod bearings, as well as for the wrist-pin bearings. The pistons are aluminum and carry three piston rings. Gaskets are used between all castings except between the cylinder block and the crankcase. Here, the surfaces are very accurately machined, and a thin film of plastic adhesive is applied before the two are joined.

Gearcase and Pump

The drive system and pump used with the powerhead described above appear in Fig. 10-3. Both the forward and reverse drive gears are continuously meshed with the pinion gear. Shifting is accomplished by moving a

FIGURE 10-1. *A typical outboard motor. (Courtesy of Evinrude Motors.)*

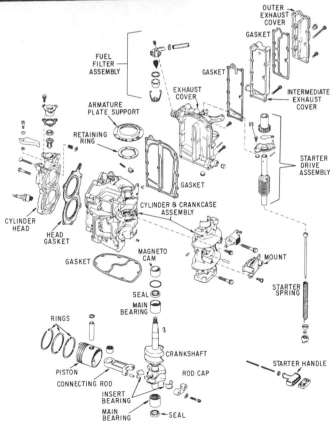

FIGURE 10-2. *Evinrude Sportwin powerhead. (Courtesy of Evinrude Motors.)*

clutch dog along the splined propeller shaft to engage the forward or reverse gear as desired. With the clutch dog in its center, or neutral position, neither gear is engaged.

The water pump is located in the upper portion of the gear case assembly, with the impeller being pinned to the drive shaft. Seals and gaskets are used wherever required to prevent water entering and lubricant leaking from the gearcase.

Ignition System

The majority of outboard motors have magneto ignition. Smaller sizes generally have flywheel magnetos. Four- and six-cylinder motors generally have removable magnetos. In this case, a ring gear on the flywheel and a similar, smaller gear on the magneto drive the magneto; the gears are coupled by a notched drive belt.

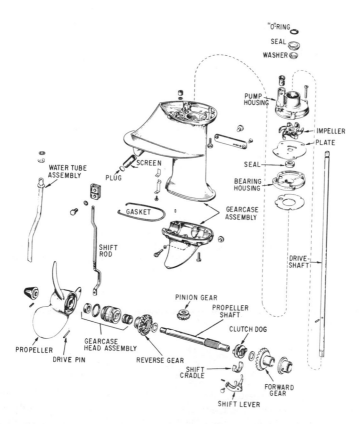

FIGURE 10-3. *Evinrude Sportwin gearcase group. (Courtesy of Evinrude Motors.)*

Fuel System

A pressure-tight crankcase is essential to two-cycles engines. Thus, single-cylinder outboards have seals at both crankshaft ends. Multicylinder outboards, which have separate, pressure-tight compartments for each cylinder, require intermediate crankshaft seals, as well as end seals. A reed valve assembly is generally used to admit the fuel mixture from the carburetor to the crankcase.

An integral fuel tank is used only on the smallest outboards, and the fuel is gravity-fed to the carburetor. The majority of outboards have separate tanks and the fuel is either pressure-fed or suction-fed from the tank to the carburetor. In the pressure-fed system, a hose applies pressure from the crankcase to the fuel tank, and a second hose carries the fuel from the tank to the carburetor. In the suction-fed system, a single hose is used. The fuel tank is vented and a diaphragm fuel pump, operated by pulsations in crankcase pressure, sucks the fuel from the tank and pumps it to the carburetor.

Starter and Electrical Systems

Most small outboards are equipped with a manual, rewind starter and simple magneto ignition, and require no electrical system.

Larger outboards are frequently equipped with an electric starter, a generator, a battery, and either magneto or battery ignition.

General Outboard Maintenance

Outboard motors require periodic maintenance if they are to operate properly and dependably and have a long useful life. The more important maintenance operations are described in this section.

Storage

Certain steps are necessary to protect the outboard motor from corrosion before it is placed in storage at the end of a boating season. The following procedure, recommended by Evinrude, will afford adequate protection and enable putting the motor back in service with a minimum of difficulty at the end of the storage period.

If the motor has been used in salt water, it should be run in fresh water for a short period.

Lubricate the internal powerhead parts. This can be done in various ways, but "fogging" described here, is the preferred method. Before lubricating, disconnect the fuel line and start the motor. With the motor running in fresh water at fast-idle, inject rust-preventive oil into the carburetor intake. Put in several good squirts, and let the motor run until the carburetor is empty of fuel. Removing fuel from the carburetor will prevent varnish or gum deposits from forming during storage.

Although not as effective, a second way to lubricate the internal parts of the powerhead is to choke the motor while it is running at about one-half throttle. Let the motor run until it chokes out and stops by itself.

After removing the motor from the water, place it in an upright position. With the throttle fully retarded and the engine in neutral, give the starter rope several slow pulls, this will remove residual water from the water pump.

Remove the fuel filter bowl and the filter element and clean them with neutral spirits. Drain and clean the fuel tank and hose. The connector housing on the tank can be removed for easier, more through cleaning.

Remove the propeller, clean and lubricate the propeller shaft, and replace the drive pin if it is worn. If the propeller is bent or nicked, repair or replace it.

Drain the gear case. If water or metal particles appear in the oil, tear down the gear case and check all parts for wear and corrosion. To guard against further entry of water, replace all seals and gaskets. Refill the gear case with the lubricant recommended by the manufacturer.

Wipe all exterior metallic parts of the motor with a lightly oiled cloth, and wax fiberglass covers.

Store the motor in an upright position in a dry, well-ventilated area. Motor stands are available, or can be constructed easily with a few two-by-fours. Do not store the motor in an air-tight container.

If the motor is equipped with electric starting, the battery should be fully charged and stored in a cool, dry place.

Fuel and Lubrication

The internal parts of the outboard motor powerhead are lubricated by oil mixed with the gasoline. Use the fuel and oil recommended by the motor manufacturer, in the ratio specified.

Where possible, fuel should be mixed in a separate container rather than in the outboard fuel tank. The mixing container should be capped when not in use. Fuel should not be mixed and stored for extended periods of time, as the fuel and oil will separate after standing for several days.

To ensure that the oil is thoroughly mixed with the gasoline, pour in half the required amount of gasoline, then add the required amount of oil. Cap the container and shake vigorously for at least one minute. Add the remaining gasoline, recap the container, and again shake vigorously for one minute.

The gearcase should be checked at frequent intervals to make certain lubricant has not been lost, or that water has not entered. One outboard manufacturer recommends that the lubricant in the lower unit be replaced at intervals not exceeding thirty days. In all cases, consult the manufacturer's instructions for the type of lubricant to be used.

On most outboards several other parts require periodic lubrication. Here again, the manufacturer's service manual should be checked to determine what parts should be lubricated and how frequently.

Dunked Outboard Treatment

Outboard motors are designed to have only the lower unit submerged under water. The powerhead is a precision piece of equipment that can be damaged if submerged. Yet, hundreds of outboards are completely submerged; either the motor is dropped in the water when it is being attached to the boat, or the clamp screws work loose while the motor is running and it is lost overboard.

If a motor is lost overboard while running, mechanical damage to such internal parts as pistons, connecting rods, and crankshaft can result, in addition to damage by corrosion. The motor should be torn down, cleaned, air-dried, and inspected for parts damage.

Motors dropped in fresh water while not operating can normally be started safely if recovered within a few hours. If sand or silt has entered the powerhead, some reconditioning is necessary before the motor can be started.

Thoroughly dry the magneto and electrical system, and disassemble and clean the carburetor before attempting to start the motor. Next, remove the spark plugs and pull the starter until all water present has been expelled. Flush the cylinders and crankcase compartments with alcohol, then squirt or spray lubricating oil into the cylinders and pull the starter to distribute the oil. Before replacing the spark plugs, clean and dry them.

Once the motor is started, listen for any unusual noises. If none are apparent, run the motor until normal operating temperature is reached. Stop and then restart the motor, and if everything appears normal, probably no permanent damage has been done.

Outboards dunked in salt water require complete disassembly of the powerhead, regardless of whether the motor was operating at the time it was submerged.

Motors retrieved from salt water should be kept submerged in cold, fresh water until they can be torn down for cleaning. This will reduce corrosion damage, since heat and oxygen accelerate corrosion. If the motor is so large that a suitable container cannot be found, remove and submerge the powerhead. Do not delay cleaning.

After disassembly, all parts should be thoroughly washed in hot, soapy water and air dried. Replace all parts showing corrosion or other damage. Also, replace any bearings which cannot be disassembled for cleaning and inspection, if there is any question as to their condition. Before reassembling the motor, thoroughly coat all mechanical parts with clean oil.

Repairing Powerheads

In many cases, faulty performance can be traced to the fuel or electrical system, and these should be checked thoroughly before disassembling the powerhead for repair.

Disassembling Powerheads

Once it has been determined that the powerhead must be torn down, remove the starter housing, flywheel, magneto assembly, and carburetor. Then remove the powerhead from the lower assembly.

Remove the cylinder head, the intake and exhaust cover plates, and then the bolts securing the cylinder block to the crankcase. Separate the block and crankcase by prying them apart, being careful not to mar the surface of either.

Next, remove the rod caps, bearing races, and bearings. Keep these parts in separate containers, marked according to the cylinders from which they were removed. The pistons and connecting rods can now be pushed out of the block. At this point, if necessary, the crankshaft and main bearings can also be lifted out of the block.

Connecting Rods

During the manufacturing process of steel connecting rods, the crank-pin end of the rod usually is split by a method called fracturing. This results in a fractured fit between the main part of the rod and the cap, and it is imperative that the rod and cap are mated properly when assembled. Refer to Fig. 10-4. When correctly assembled, the lines of fracture almost disappear. Rod cap screws should always be torqued to the manufacturer's specifications.

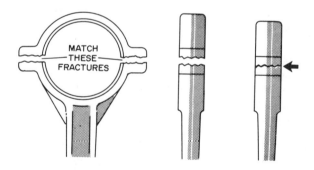

FIGURE 10-4. *Matching cap to connecting rod. (Courtesy of McCulloch Corp.)*

With aluminum connecting rods the mating surfaces of the rod and cap are milled rather than fractured, and each has a dot or other identifying mark on one side. When installing the cap, locate it so that the dots are on the same surface of the rod assembly. Caps should not be interchanged between rods.

It is also important that rods be turned in the proper position on the crankpin. On McCulloch engines, for example, the word top, or the oil hole, which appears in the channel in each rod, should face the top or flywheel end of the motor. Installed in this manner, oil will collect in the rod channel and flow into the oil hole to lubricate either the crank- or wrist-pin bearings.

Bearings

Roller and needle bearings are widely used as connecting rod, main, and wrist-pin bearings in outboard motors. Connecting rod and main bearings of this type may be caged or uncaged. Rollers and cages, where used, must be kept separated, and parts must not be interchanged between cylinders. When assembling bearings and cages, use grease to hold the rollers in place. Also, carefully match the cage halves by mating and identifying the groove cut into one edge of the cage. See Fig. 10-5. One roller fits into each slot in the cage and one fits between each end of the cage halves.

FIGURE 10-5. *Matching cage halves.*
(Courtesy of McCulloch Corp.)

Roller or needle wrist-pin bearings are generally assembled as a replaceable unit. When replacement is required, the connecting rod and piston are separated by removing the wrist pin. The wrist-pin bearing may then be pressed out and a replacement pressed in. Chilling the wrist pin in dry ice will make it easier to press into the rod or piston.

In some engines, ball bearings are used as the outer main bearings. In this case, a puller is required to remove the bearings from the crankshaft, and a press is used to install the replacement bearings.

Sometimes bronze bushings are used as main bearings. In a two-piece crankcase construction with a detachable cylinder block, the main bearings often are cast integrally with the crankcase sections. If the bearings are excessively worn, the two-piece crankcase must be replaced.

Main Bearing Seals

To maintain pressure-tight crankcase compartments, a seal is required at each end of the crankcase and between adjacent compartments. End seals are generally rubber, while the inner seals between adjacent crankcase

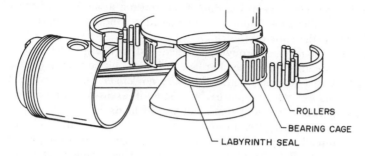

FIGURE 10-6. *Labyrinth type seal. (Courtesy of McCulloch Corp.)*

sections vary in materials. Through 1963, for example, some Scott outboard motors used a labyrinth seal with the center main bearings. Labyrinth seals consist of grooves cut in the crankshaft immediately above and below the center main-bearing journal, as shown in Fig. 10-6.

Later motors have teflon-center main-bearing seals. As shown in Fig. 10-7, the main bearings are grooved on the lower edge to accommodate this kind of seal. During installation the teflon seal should be positioned so that the cut ends are not at the point where the block and crankcase come together.

Pistons and Rings

Aluminum pistons fitted with either two or three rings are commonly used in outboard motors. In some instances, pins are pressed into openings

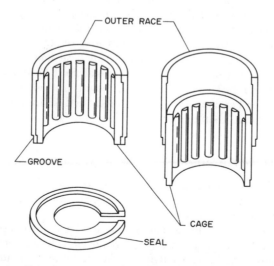

FIGURE 10-7. *Teflon-type seal. (Courtesy of McCulloch Corp.)*

in the ring grooves to keep the rings from shifting around the piston during operation. In this case, the rings are placed on the piston with the "ring pin" between the ends of the ring.

Pistons should be thoroughly cleaned and then inspected to determine if they are suitable for reuse. Replace cracked, chipped, or scored pistons and pistons that are worn until the skirt no longer fits the cylinder with proper clearance. Also, replace the piston if excessive side clearance is measured between the new rings and piston lands.

In some engines, the piston rings are identical, but each must be installed correctly, top to bottom. On Scott engines, for example, the top inner edges of all three rings are beveled. This beveled edge must be installed toward the dome of the piston. Follow the manufacturer's recommendations in selecting replacement rings.

Thoroughly oil rings and piston. Use a ring compressor to insert the piston and rings into the cylinder.

Block and Crankcase

On many outboards, the cylinder block and crankcase are matched assemblies and must be replaced as such. Frequently, the cylinder sleeves are cast with the block and cannot be replaced. However, if the cylinder walls show slight evidence of damage they may be cleaned up with a finishing hone used with a drill press. Normally, no more than 0.005 in. should be removed with the hone.

If the damage cannot be remedied by honing, the block can be rebored to a standard oversize and fitted with oversize pistons. (Note: in this case, all cylinders must be bored to the same diameter, even if only one is damaged. This is essential, to maintain equal displacement and preserve the mechanical balance of the engine.)

Before reassembling, thoroughly clean the mating surfaces of the cylinder block and crankcase. Slight nicks and scratches can be removed by lapping on a lapping block or glass plate. Use fine emery paper, and replace parts if an excessive amount of material must be removed.

Generally, no gasket is used at this point. Instead, a gasket cement, such as Gastite or Permatex, is applied lightly and uniformly to the mating surfaces, taking care that the adhesive does not flow into the bearings or crankcase passages.

Reassembling the Powerhead

In general, the reassembly of the powerhead is the reverse of the disassembly procedure. Replace all gaskets used, and tighten all bolts to the manufacturer's recommended torque.

When the cylinder block and crankcase have been assembled, turn the crankshaft by hand (spark plugs removed). If all parts have been reinstalled correctly, the crankshaft should turn easily. If any catching or binding is observed, the powerhead should be disassembled and thoroughly checked.

Repairing the Lower Assembly

The lower motor assembly is comprised of two, three, or more, separate castings, which contain the drive system components, pump and water lines, and the exhaust discharge line. The lower assembly of the Scott outboard shown in Fig. 10-8, consists of a lower motor casing, a pump housing, and a lower unit.

The lower motor casing is also referred to as an exhaust housing or as a drive-shaft housing, and the lower unit is frequently called the gearcase, for the obvious reason that it contains the pinion and drive gears. The gearcase is frequently a two-piece construction, with the pump mounted in the upper section.

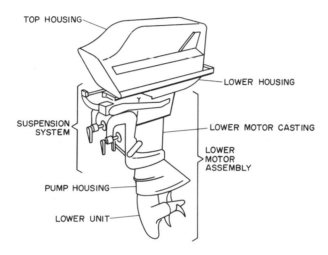

FIGURE 10-8. *Sport Scott outboard motor. (Courtesy of McCulloch Corp.)*

External Castings

Aluminum alloys are generally used for the lower motor assembly castings. Before aluminum parts are painted, they receive a uniform coating of aluminum oxide over the surface. This anodized layer is quite resistant to corrosion; and, additionally, paint bonds much better to an anodized surface than to bare aluminum. When working with outboards, care must be taken not to scratch the surface, for this will expose the bare metal to corrosion damage. For touchup, paint is available in spray cans (matching colors) from the motor manufacturers.

Also, the machined surfaces of casting must not be nicked or scratched, otherwise an oil or water leak will result. All old gaskets must be thoroughly removed and replaced with new gaskets during assembly. Where gaskets are not specified, apply a thin, uniform coat of a sealer compound to the mating surfaces.

All bolts or screws should be run down snugly and then alternately tightened to the torque specified by the manufacturer.

Lower Motor Casing

Typically, the lower motor casing houses the upper shift mechanism, the water cooling lines, and the driveshaft. Some outboards have a bailer pump in addition to the customary cooling pump, and in this case, the lower motor casing will also contain bailer pump lines.

Ordinarily, the lower motor casing will need to be removed only for replacement if it should be damaged. The following procedure explains how this is done in the case of a typical outboard. Such as the 28-hp Sport Scott:

Remove the inspection plate on the lower port side of the lower motor casing and disconnect the upper and lower shift rods (Fig. 10-9).

Remove the four allen-head screws securing the pump housing to the lower motor casing and pull this assembly down and out of the lower motor casing (Fig. 10-9).

Disconnect the throttle linkage, then the fuel lines from the fuel pump.

Remove the front bracket snubber and the two bolts securing the front mount bracket to the powerhead.

Remove the twelve screws securing the powerhead to the lower motor casing, and separate the two assemblies.

Disconnect the lower motor casing from the upper and lower rubber mounts; then remove the shift mechanism, water lines, and rubber mounts.

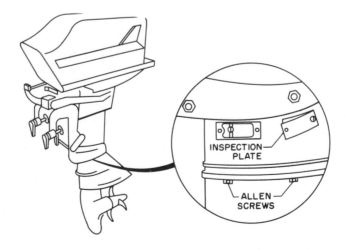

FIGURE 10-9. *Separation of pump housing from lower motor casing. (Courtesy of McCulloch Corp.)*

During assembly, reverse the steps given above for disassembly, taking the following precautions.

Be sure to install the water line in the recessed slot at the top of the motor casing.

Use a new lower motor casing to powerhead gasket.

Lubricate the seals in the water and bailer pumps. Guide the lower unit and pump housing into the lower motor casing, making certain that the water and bailer lines fit snugly into the rubber seals in the two pumps.

Tighten the pump housing to lower motor housing screws to a torque of 200 inch-pounds, and the powerhead mounting screws to 80 inch-pounds.

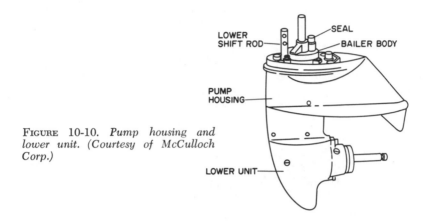

FIGURE 10-10. *Pump housing and lower unit. (Courtesy of McCulloch Corp.)*

Pump Housing and Lower Unit

The pump housing and lower unit used on the Sport Scott are shown in Fig. 10-10. The pump housing serves as a support between the lower motor casing and the lower unit. It contains the water and bailer pump assemblies, driveshaft, and a driveshaft bearing and seal.

The lower unit on this motor uses a vertical shift mechanism. A fork attached to the lower shift rod positions the clutch dog on the splined lower part of the driveshaft. The clutch dog is moved down, and engages the lower, or forward, gear when the shift lever is moved to the forward position. When the shift lever is moved to reverse, the clutch dog is moved upward and engages the upper, or reverse gear. See Fig. 10-11.

The shift mechanism can be adjusted by removing the bearing cap and observing the position of the clutch dog in relation to the forward and reverse gears. If correctly positioned, the clutch dog should be midway between the two gears, with the shift lever in the neutral position. Should adjustment be required, remove the inspection plate from the lower port side of the motor casing, and remove the two screws connecting the upper and lower shift rods (Fig. 10-9). Turn the lower shift rod to adjust the position of the clutch dog.

Where disassembly is required for servicing, the steps below should be followed in the order given:

Remove the pump housing and lower unit from the lower motor casing, and drain the lubricant from the lower unit.

Remove the two screws which secure the lower unit bearing cap (Fig. 10-11), and pull the bearing cap assembly out of the lower unit.

If required, the propeller shaft, pinion gear, and two thrust bearings can be removed from the bearing cap, as follows.

First, bend the washer (located under the pinion nut) flat, and remove the pinion nut, gear, and key. Next, press the propeller shaft, seal, and

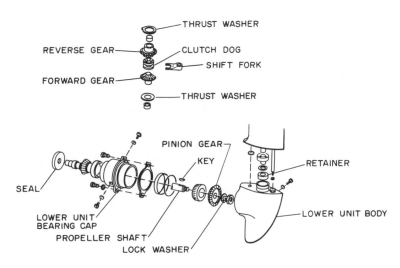

FIGURE 10-11. *Exploded view of lower unit. (Courtesy of McCulloch Corp.)*

reverse thrust bearing out of the bearing cap. Press the propeller shaft from the pinion gear end. Now, the front and rear bearing cups can be removed and installed using tools No. J7533-1 and No. J7533-2 (available from McCulloch). Replace bearings and cups in *sets* only. When assembling the pinion gear, tighten the nut until there is a slight drag when the propeller shaft is turned. Do not allow end play or excessive preload on the bearings. Bend the washer up around the pinion gear nut.

Remove the pump assembly mounting screws and slide each pump off separately, taking care not to damage the seals in the driveshaft holes of the pumps as they pass over the splines of the driveshaft. Be certain to remove the impeller drive pins from the slots in the driveshaft.

To separate the pump housing and lower unit, remove the two allen-head screws at the bottom of the pump housing. Remove the pin which secures the retainer to the driveshaft, and then the driveshaft.

At this point, the forward and reverse gears can be lifted out.

If the following bearings or seals require replacement, use these special tools, which are available from the manufacturer: forward gear roller bearing—J7531; reverse, gear roller bearing—J7530; pump housing bushing —7529; pump housing, upper driveshaft seal—J7552.

Replace any worn or damaged parts, and assemble in the reverse order. During assembly, make certain that all seals are in place and in good condition and that the forward and reverse gear thrust washers are keyed in position, with the bronze surface facing the gears.

Install the shift rod, shift fork, and gears; then align the clutch dog in the unit and insert the driveshaft.

When assembling the lower unit and pump housing, be certain the thrust washer, driveshaft retainer ring, and all seals are in place.

Use Loctite A, or a similar locking agent, on the pump housing to lower unit allen-head screws; torque the screws to 200 inch-pounds.

Guide the water pump into position and install the impeller with the word "top" toward the open end of the water pump. Be certain that the vinyl tape is fastened to the water-pump mounting bosses.

Position the round separator plate and large "O" ring seal in the water-pump body, then slide the remaining separator plate into position.

Install the bailer impeller with the word "top" toward the bailer cavity. The word "top," on the impeller blades, should not be visible. Fit the small "O" ring seal in the groove around the bailer pump cavity.

Guide the bailer assembly into place. Be certain the impeller drive pin is in place. Secure the assembly to the pump housing.

Guide the entire assembly into the lower motor casing. Be certain the water and bailer lines mate correctly with the seals in the water and bailer pump. Torque the pump housing to lower unit screws to 200 inch-pounds.

Connect the upper and lower shift rods. Test for full clutch dog engagement by placing the shift in forward and reverse. If the clutch dog does not fully engage one or the other gear, remove the two shift rod coupling screws and turn the lower shift rod to adjust. In the "neutral" position, the clutch dog should be centered without touching either gear.

With the motor in an upright position, fill the lower unit with EP No. 90 outboard gear lubricant. Fill through the fill plug until lubricant reaches the level of the fill plug hole. The capacity is 7 ounces.

CHAPTER *11*

Troubleshooting and Tuneup

In servicing engines, it is generally necessary first to determine which unit or part is defective, and then to replace or adjust the part.

The ability to quickly and accurately diagnose engine troubles is essential to a serviceman's success. Fortunately, this ability is not difficult to acquire, providing one understands the engine operation, including carburetion and ignition.

Troubleshooting Inoperative Engines

One of the most common engine complaints is total failure to run; this failure can be caused by a wider range of defects than any other engine trouble. For these reasons, detailed procedures will now be given for troubleshooting inoperative engines. With the understanding gained here, there should be little difficulty in understanding the somewhat abbreviated procedures given later for diagnosing other engine complaints.

Isolating the Trouble

Before a gasoline engine can be started, it must have sufficient compression in the cylinder, a proper fuel-air mixture, and an ignition spark, properly timed, to fire the mixture. In troubleshooting an inoperative engine, the repairman should first determine whether the failure is due to a compression loss or to an ignition or fuel system malfunction.

To determine if a reasonable amount of compression exists, slowly crank the engine by hand; a springy resistance should be felt at some point as the engine is turned. On single-cylinder, two-cycle engines, resistance should be felt at some point during every crankshaft revolution; on single-cylinder, four-cycle engines, it should be felt only on alternate revolutions. In any event, if the engine turns freely and there is little or no resistance at any point, most likely a compression loss is preventing the engine from starting. Compression loss can be caused by a blown head gasket, a cracked piston, badly worn piston rings, or a badly burned, broken or stuck valve. Occasionally, low compression will result from inadequate cylinder lubrication. This may be due to engine overheating or to operating with insufficient lubricating oil. On a new engine or one that has not been operated for some time, the oil may have drained from the rings and cylinder so that a proper seal no longer exists. To remedy this condition, remove the spark plug and pour a small quantity of clean oil into the cylinder. Crank the engine over several times to distribute the oil over the cylinder wall; then replace the spark plug and recheck the compression. If this does not restore compression, the engine must then be partially disassembled to determine the cause of low compression.

If the compression appears to be satisfactory, remove and inspect the spark plug. If the insulator is broken, or if the plug appears to be fouled or soaked with oil, it should be replaced. If it is reasonably dry and clean, check the electrode gap. Depending upon the engine, the gap should be approximately 0.025 in.

To check the output from the ignition system, hold the spark plug lead about 1/8 in. from the cylinder head, while cranking the engine with the ignition switch on. If a spark is produced, the trouble is probably not in the ignition system. If little or no spark is produced, it will be necessary to check the ignition system to pinpoint and correct the trouble. (Note: To avoid electrical shock while checking ignition system output, connect the ignition lead to the spark plug and temporarily open the electrode gap to 1/8 in. Lay the metal shell of the plug on the cylinder head (or other engine ground) and check for a spark at the electrodes as the engine is cranked. Before installing the plug, reset the gap.)

If the spark plug appeared saturated with gasoline when first removed, the engine may have been flooded by excessive choking. Check the carburetor to see that the choke valve is open; then crank the engine over several times before replacing the plug. This will blow the excess fuel from the combustion chamber. Dry the old plug before it is replaced, or use a new plug.

A bone dry plug generally indicates that no fuel is reaching the combustion chamber. In this case, before replacing the plug, pour a teaspoonful of gasoline through the spark plug hole. Crank the engine, and if it fires or starts and runs for a few seconds, the trouble definitely stems from the fuel system.

Locating Battery Ignition Defects

If the battery-ignition system produces little or no spark, the trouble may be in the battery, the ignition switch, the coil, the breaker points, the condenser, the spark plug, or the circuit wiring. On multicylinder engines, the defect may also be in the distributor cap or rotor.

If the engine has an electrical starter, and the starter operates satisfactorily, the battery can be eliminated as the cause of ignition failure. If there is no starter, check the battery with a hydrometer or substitute a good battery whose voltage rating is the same as that of the engine battery.

If the battery checks out, check the ignition points. Burned, badly pitted points should be replaced. Dirty points should be cleaned. Also check the gap setting, making certain the points open and close as the engine is cranked. If they do not and if the ignition cam does not turn, then there is mechanical trouble in the camshaft, timing gear, or distributor drive.

With the ignition switch on, notice whether a spark occurs at the points as they open. If not, either the ignition switch or primary winding of the coil may be open-circuited or the condenser may be short-circuited.

To check the ignition switch, run a wire from the ungrounded terminal of the battery to the input terminal of the ignition coil. If this corrects the trouble, replace the switch. Otherwise, check the coil with a coil tester, if available. If not, use an ohmmeter to check the primary winding for an open circuit. With the ignition switch off or with one primary lead disconnected from the coil, the resistance between the primary terminals of the coil normally should be no more than 5 ohms.

Defective coils can also be detected by substituting a good coil. For test purposes, an exact replacement is not required. However, the voltage rating of the substitute coil must be the same as the one being checked. If the substitute coil produces an output voltage, the old coil is defective and should be replaced.

If the coil is good, temporarily disconnect the condenser from the breaker points. If the condenser is shorted, a spark will appear when the points open. For a conclusive check, a condenser tester can be used. However, a shorted condenser will generally show up on an ohmmeter test. Again, a new condenser can be substituted for the one that is suspected.

Where a distributor cap and rotor are used, check for a spark by holding the secondary coil lead 1/8 in. from the engine while it is being cranked. If a spark appears at this point but not at the spark plugs, remove and inspect both the cap and rotor. Replace either or both if they show signs of arcing or burning. If not, substitute a new rotor, and if this doesn't correct the trouble, try a new distributor cap.

Checking Magnetos

Like battery ignition systems, magnetos are also subject to breaker point, condenser, and coil failure. However, magnetos are subject to some additional troubles as well, such as excessive air gap, impulse coupling failure, and infrequently, weak magnets.

When a removable magneto fails to produce sufficient output for engine starting, first check the impulse coupling. Crank the engine slowly and listen for the characteristic snap as the coupling releases. If no snap is heard, the magneto should be removed, and the coupling cleaned and then checked for worn or broken parts. (Spring breakage is common in impulse couplings.)

If the impulse coupling is operating properly, check the magneto. Removable and flywheel magnetos are checked in approximately the same way. To check the condition and operation of breaker points in a removable magneto, the magneto cover must first be removed, as shown in Fig. 11-1. In some flywheel magnetos, the points and condenser are also mounted externally, the points being driven from the engine camshaft. In most cases, however, the flywheel must be removed to gain access to the breaker points in flywheel magnetos.

Regardless of the magneto type, the points should be checked for proper gap, burning, and an oily or dirty surface. Dirt and oil can be removed by drawing a piece of hard paper between the points. Slight burning can be corrected with a fine-cut file, after which the gap must be checked. Badly burned points should be replaced, and in this case, the condenser as well, since point burning is frequently caused by a condenser that has lost capacitance.

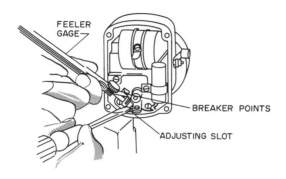

FIGURE 11-1. *Adjusting breaker points on a removable magneto. (Courtesy of Wisconsin Motor Corp.)*

A short circuit sometimes occurs between the stationary and moving portions of the breaker point set. This may be due to a worn insulating bushing in the moving breaker, which slips over the pin fixed to the stationary point. Or the insulator at the breaker point terminal may be broken or assembled incorrectly, so that the flat spring of the moving breaker touches the grounded stationary contact assembly.

An ohmmeter, or a battery and test lamp, can be used to determine if the points are shorted; disconnect the coil lead from the breaker point terminal and then connect the ohmmeter or test lamp between the breaker terminal and ground. Crank the engine until the points are open and note the resistance. A short circuit is indicated by a zero ohmmeter reading or by lighting of the test lamp. If the circuit is shorted, disconnect the engine stop-switch lead from the breaker point terminal. If the short is still present, disconnect the condenser lead and check again. If the short is still present, replace the points. If the short is in the stop switch, the wiring and switch should be checked to determine which is at fault. If the condenser is shorted, it should be replaced.

If the trouble is not in the breaker points, check the condenser and coil in that order. Condenser and coil testers should be used if available; otherwise, an ohmmeter can be used to determine if the condenser is shorted or if the primary winding of a coil is open. In some cases, however, the results of ohmmeter tests on coils and condensers will not be conclusive. Again, as in the case of battery ignition, coils and condensers that are known to be good can be substituted for units that are suspected of being defective.

Weak magnets are seldom the cause of a magneto going completely dead. A weak magnet will reduce magneto output, but magnets do not suddenly lose their magnetism for no reason, particularly alnico and ceramic magnets, now used almost universally in magnetos.

Weak magnets are frequently the result of the owner's or amateur mechanic's attempt to recharge a perfectly good magnet, when the trouble actually was in the points, coil, or condenser, or maybe not even in the magneto at all.

Excessive air gap between the poles of the magneto armature and the flywheel, or rotor, can drastically reduce magneto output voltage. Here again, this is not likely to happen suddenly in a magneto that has been operating satisfactorily. Far more likely, someone has removed the coil and armature assembly while trying to find the original trouble, and bolted them back without realizing the importance of correct air-gap adjustment. Again, the armature screws may have worked loose, allowing it to shift away from its proper position.

In addition to the above, magneto air gap must be reset whenever the coil is removed for testing or replacement. The manufacturer's service literature should be checked for the recommended procedure and specified gap width. In most cases, the specified air gap will lie in the range of 0.006 to 0.020 in. In general, the armature screws should be loosened and a feeler gauge (or piece of shim stock of the specified thickness) inserted between the armature poles and flywheel, or rotor. The armature should be held tightly against the gauge while the screws are being tightened. The gauge should then be removed. (Note: In some magnetos the air gap is not adjustable.)

A bent crankshaft, warped flywheel, or excessively worn main bearing may make it impossible to obtain the correct air gap without having the flywheel rub the armature at some point in its rotation. In this case, of course, the worn or damaged part must be replaced before a satisfactory air gap adjustment can be made.

Checking Fuel Systems

If an engine refuses to start, and the compression and ignition both appear satisfactory, it will then be necessary to examine the fuel system.

Begin by checking to see that there is plenty of suitable fuel in the tank, and remember that what *appears* to be gasoline may actually be kerosene, paint thinner, or even water. If the fuel tank contents are questionable drain and refill with fresh, clean gasoline, or in two-cycle engines, with a suitable mixture of fuel and oil.

Make certain the fuel shutoff valve is fully open; that the carburetor and fuel pump, if used, are tightly bolted to the engine and that the controls are properly connected to the throttle and choke valves.

Correct anything that may be found wrong in preliminary checks, and then try to start the engine. If it starts, let it reach operating temperature, and then test for high- and low-speed operation. Readjust the carburetor as required.

If the engine does not start, then disconnect the fuel line at the carburetor to see that adequate fuel is reaching the carburetor. In gravity-fed systems, the fuel should flow in a continuous stream. If little or no fuel flows from the line, remove the line and check to see whether it, a fuel filter, or a fitting is obstructed. A simple check can be made by blowing through the line. If a line or fitting is tightly blocked, use compressed air to clear the obstruction. If a compressor is not available, an ordinary hand-operated tire pump will suffice.

On engines that have a fuel pump, the absence of fuel at the carburetor may be due to a defective pump, a leak or obstruction between the tank and pump, or an obstruction in the line from the pump to the carburetor. Disconnect the line from the tank at the pump end; if fuel cannot be sucked from the line, the line is either obstructed or has an air leak at some point. If fuel is reaching the pump, remove and check the outlet line. If this line is in good condition, it will be necessary to repair or replace the pump.

If a satisfactory supply of fuel is reaching the carburetor and the engine doesn't run, check the high- and low-speed adjusting screws to see that both are set from one to one-and-one-half turns from their maximum clockwise position. If the engine now starts, let it reach operating temperature, then make a final carburetor adjustment.

If the engine still doesn't start after setting the high and low-speed adjustments, the carburetor should be removed, and serviced.

In two-cycle engines, the reed valve should always be checked, as a defective reed valve can keep the engine from operating. The carburetor must be removed to inspect or replace the reed valve assembly, so if the carburetor appears to be in good condition when torn down, remove and inspect the reed valve to see that it closes properly and opens freely before reinstalling the carburetor.

Troubleshooting Other Engine Complaints

Other engine complaints are localized in about the same way as failure of an engine to start. Indeed, many of the complaints which will now be discussed are caused by the same troubles as were covered in the case of an inoperative engine.

Hard Starting

Hard starting may be due to a partial compression loss, or a defect in the ignition or fuel systems. Other causes are stale fuel, which no longer vaporizes easily; a defective starter, which does not spin the engine properly; and, in two-cycle engines, worn main bearings or faulty crankshaft seals.

Note whether the starter cranks the engine at what appears to be a reasonable starting speed. If too slow, check the battery, starter, solenoid, and cables.

Excessive cranking speed sometimes indicates a serious loss of compression. If available, check the compression with a compression gauge. For most engines in good condition, the compression should be at least 100 pounds per square inch. If the compression is lower than this, the engine should be checked to determine the cause of a reduced compression.

Clean and gap the spark plug or, preferably, replace it and again check for proper starting. If the plug is in good condition or has been replaced, check the ignition voltage to the spark plug, as outlined previously. If it appears weak, further tests should be made on the ignition system. If it appears normal, check the fuel system.

Check to see that fresh, clean fuel of the proper type is being used. Make certain that the choke works properly, that there are no carburetor or manifold air leaks, and then check the carburetor adjustment. If this doesn't correct the trouble, the carburetor should be cleaned and, if used, the reed valve inspected. In a two-cycle engine, defective crankcase seals are far more likely to produce hard starting than total failure to start.

Loss of Power

In this complaint, note whether the engine also overheats, for serious overheating in itself will cause a drastic reduction of engine power. If the power loss is accompanied by overheating, check for adequate lubrication, and determine whether the flow of air through the shroud and around the cylinder is obstructed by dirt or trash. On water-cooled engines, check for a defective thermostat or water pump or an obstructed water passage. Improper ignition timing will also cause overheating and a loss of power.

If the power loss is not accompanied by overheating, check compression, ignition, and carburetion in that order. Remember, too, that a dirty air cleaner can result in a drastic reduction in engine power, as can a partially closed choke valve.

In two-cycle engines, power loss is frequently caused by an accumulation of carbon in the exhaust ports. Power loss also is caused by a fouled or sluggish reed valve or by defective crankcase seals.

Erratic Operation

With engines that surge or run unevenly, the trouble usually is found in either the fuel system or governor mechanism.

If the fuel system is causing trouble, and there is evidence of flooding, such as fuel dripping from the carburetor, or very black exhaust smoke, the float level may be set too high or the float valve may be stuck. Generally the carburetor must be disassembled to correct the float level or the valve operation, although sometimes lightly tapping the float bowl with a screwdriver handle will free a stuck float valve. Whenever the carburetor is disassembled, both the float valve operation and the float level should be checked.

Before removing the carburetor, however, check both the high- and low-speed mixture adjustments. Also check the throttle valve and throttle linkage for binding.

To determine whether the governor is at fault, disconnect it from the throttle linkage and control the throttle manually. If the engine then runs evenly, clean and oil the governor assembly and check for binding.

Cylinder Miss

When a cylinder continuously misses in a multicylinder engine, the trouble most frequently is a defective spark plug. However, a defective distributor cap or bad spark-plug leads can produce the same effect.

If plug replacement does not correct the problem and if plenty of ignition voltage is reaching the offending cylinder (proving the distributor cap and ignition leads are satisfactory), the compression should be checked. If very low compression is found on the missing cylinder in comparison to the others, there are internal engine problems, such as burned valves, a blown head-gasket, broken rings, or a defective piston. On two-cycle, multicylinder engines, the trouble may also be one or more defective inlet reeds or a defective crankcase seal.

Single cylinder engines cannot miss continuously, but may "skip" occasionally, due to a bad spark plug, burned or sticking breaker points, a poor condenser, or a loose connection at some point in the ignition circuit. An occasional miss also may be due to a sticking valve, to dirty fuel, or to an improperly adjusted carburetor.

Knocks

Engine "knocks" can be caused by excessive wear in internal moving parts, particularly those parts that move with reciprocating rather than rotary motion. Also, engine knocks frequently are due to excessively advanced ignition timing and to carbon accumulation in the combustion chamber.

FIGURE 11-2. *A likely cause of vibration in outboards. (Courtesy of Evinrude Motors.)*

The experienced repairman often can identify the source of engine noises by their characteristic sound. Thus, excessive valve tappet clearance produces a click, while worn connecting-rod bearings produce a rapping sound. Slightly loose rod bearings make a sound similar to piston slap or worn wrist-pin bushings; badly worn rod bearings produce a hammering sound that can be heard at both high and low engine speeds. Worn main bearings make a deep thud which is loudest at low speed. A loose flywheel can produce a noise similar to the main bearing knock, but the sound may come and go from time to time. Before tearing down an engine that knocks, the repairman should make certain that the flywheel is tightly bolted to the crankshaft.

In multicylinder engines, sometimes the noise can be isolated by shorting out the spark plugs, one by one. If shorting a particular plug produces a drastic change in the knock, then trouble is indicated in the parts associated with that cylinder. In some cases, connecting-rod knock will completely disappear when the associated plug is shorted. In other cases it will still be heard but not as loudly as before. Quite frequently wrist-pin noise will actually be louder when the plug is shorted.

In some cases a stethoscope can be used to locate the source of engine knocks. Thus, valve noises will be loudest near the valve chamber, while piston and wrist-pin noises will be loudest on the side of the cylinder. Connecting-rod and main-bearing noises will appear louder at the crankcase.

Once it has been determined that the noise is due to internal trouble, the engine should be torn down and the various parts checked for wear or damage.

Vibration

Excessive vibration can be caused by either an engine defect or trouble in the unit being driven. In either case, it is caused by inbalance in a rotating part or assembly.

Likely causes of engine inbalance are bent crankshafts, warped flywheels, and flywheels with broken fins.

On a rotary lawn mower, a badly unbalanced blade will cause engine vibration, while on outboard motors, damaged propellers produce the same effect. (See Fig. 11-2.)

Frequently, only a thorough outward inspection is necessary to determine the cause of excessive vibration. Sometimes, however, the engine must be torn down and the internal parts checked. This would be necessary, for example, when a portion of the skirt of one piston has been broken away, leaving the remainder of the piston intact and operating.

Engine Tuneup

Generally, a tuneup is requested because an engine no longer performs satisfactorily. It may be hard to start, have poor high- or low-speed performance, fail to idle properly, miss, or use an excessive amount of fuel.

Tuneup includes checking the compression and ignition timing, and doing whatever is required to restore the ignition and fuel systems to good operating condition. Ideally, tuneup should also include engine cleaning and then a thorough check to see that all nuts and screws are in place and properly tightened.

Compression Check

The compression should be checked on all cylinders, using a compression gauge. If a reading lower than the minimum specified by the engine manufacturer is noted on all cylinders, or if there is a compression variation of 20 per cent or more between cylinders, the engine needs an overhaul rather than a tuneup.

Ignition System

Check all spark plugs, and service or replace any that do not appear to be in good condition. Clean and inspect the distributor cap and rotor (if used), and check spark plug wires for cracks in the insulation.

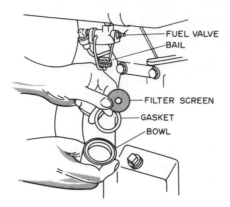

FUEL VALVE
BAIL
FILTER SCREEN
GASKET
BOWL

FIGURE 11-3. *Sediment bowl removed for cleaning. (Courtesy of Wisconsin Motor Corp.)*

Check the breaker points and if badly burned replace both the points and condenser. Slightly burned or dirty points should be filed or cleaned as described earlier. Make certain the point gap is set to the manufacturer's specifications, and then check the ignition timing.

Fuel System

Clean the air cleaner and check the fuel system for leaks. Depending upon the type, clean or replace the fuel filter (Fig. 11-3). Make certain the throttle and choke controls are properly connected at the carburetor.

Allow the engine to reach operating temperature and then set the high- and low-speed mixture adjustments, as well as the idle adjustment. If the carburetor adjustments cannot be satisfactorily made, remove and clean the carburetor, replacing any worn or damaged parts.

Upon completion of the tuneup, the engine should be tested for proper starting and operation under load.

Index

Index

Piston rings, 14
   replacement, 101-103, 112, 127, 128
Points, breaker, 62, 63, 137, 144
Powerhead
   assembly, 128
   bearings, 126
   block and crankcase, 128
   connecting rods, 125, 126
   pistons, 127, 128
   rings, 127, 128
   seals, 126, 127
Pump housing, 131, 132

Rectifiers, 83

Seat, valve, 20-22
Self inductance, 54
Spark plug
   construction, 72-73
   heat range, 73-74
   service, 74, 135, 141, 143
Speed control, 33-35
   air vane governor, 34
   centrifugal governor, 35
Starter
   manual, 75, 76
   electrical, 77-81
Suction carburetor, 31, 32, 37, 38, 40

Tank, fuel, 29, 43, 44
   repair, 43, 44
Tappet clearance, 99, 100

Timing
   ignition, 64, 65
   valve, 23
Troubleshooting, engine, 134-144
Tuneup, 143, 144

Valve service, 141
   guide replacement, 95
   lapping, 97, 98
   reconditioning, 94, 95
   removal, 93, 94
   replacement, 100
   seat, 96
   tappet clearance, 99, 100, 142

Valve system
   adjustment, 22, 23
   clearance, 22
   exhaust, 19, 20-22
   face, 20
   grinder, 22
   guide, 20-22
   intake, 19, 20-22
   keeper, 20-22
   lifter, 22, 23
   port, 20
   retainer, 20-22
   seat, 20-22
   spring, 20
   timing, 23
Vibration, 143
Voltage, 50, 136
   regulator, 86, 87

Wrist pin, 15